Copyright 2021 © Frater Acher

All rights reserved

Without limiting the rights under copyright reserved above, no part of this publication may be reproduced, stored in, or introduced into a retrieval system, or transmitted, in any form or by any means (electronic, mechanical, photocopying, recording or otherwise) without prior permission of the copyright owner and the publisher of this book.

Published by TaDehent Books 2021 Exeter UK

ISBN 978-1-911134-57-2

All images by José Gabriel Alegría Sabogal (unless credited otherwise)

Copyedited by Christopher Volpe

Cover design & typeset by Frater Acher

In memoriam

Karl von Eckartshausen

(1752–1803)

Rosicrucian Magic

A Reader on Becoming Alike to the Angelic Mind

Frater Acher

INTEGRITY is not something we strive to achieve for the gods or for other people. It is not at all a social good. Yet it is the most essential of all magical capabilities: To let each of our decisions count, as if we were standing on the scales of Ma'at. In this very moment, and then in the next. And yet not to become self-judging or rigid, but to stay connected to the flowing tides of life, like fire does.
What an exquisite challenge.

·

This book is an open
invitation. To walk
with me, on the
narrow trail of
Rosicrucian
Magic.

Frater Acher

Contents

Instead of an Introduction   1

On the Rose and the Cross

Finding access to the symbol of the rosicross through the biography and writings of Johan Valentin Andreae

Chapter 1   21

Entering the Temple. Entering the World.

Speaking Ma'at. Doing Ma'at.

Becoming Gold.

Exploring the nature of Late Medieval white magic, the cure it could become to rebalancing the scales, and the importance of an everyday lens

Chapter 2   57

Authentically Angelic

Discussing four essential premises of human apotheosis as implicitly encountered in the tradition of white magic from Johannes Trithemius onwards

Chapter 3   69

An Angelic Prayer by Karl von Eckartshausen

Introducing a mystical prayer related to the motto of the highest grade of the Order of the Golden and Rosy Cross, both in its German form and English translation

Chapter 4   75

Bernhard Schleiß von Löwenfeld: Der höchste symbolische Grad der Magie. Ein hinterlassenes Manuskript eines Weisen an seinen Sohn.

Providing the full German original text of this secret document relating to the highest Magus grade of the Order of the Golden and Rosy Cross

Chapter 4 93

Bernhard Schleiß von Löwenfeld: The highest Symbolic Grade of Magic. A manuscript left behind by a wise man to his son.

Providing a carefully annotated, complete English translation of the previous document

Chapter 5 111

The highest Symbolic Grade of Magic – A Ritual Analysis

Offering the first in-depth analysis of the above ritual, focussing on its structure and content as well as its historic ties to Ancient Jewish mysticism as well as Rosicrucian Magic

Chapter 6 147

Rosicrucian Magic – A Manifesto

Synthesising our findings on white magic into a succinct programmatic call to approaching ritual magic through the spirit of the Early Rosicrucian adepts

Chapter 7 155

On Prudence combined with Virtue by Karl von Eckartshausen

Capturing timeless wisdom on everyday ethics and noble conduct, derived from the Rosicrucian spirit of inner reformation

Chapter 8 167

J.B. Kerning and the Inner Fulcrum of *I AM*

Shining a light on an almost forgotten adept and his influential system of letter and sound magic, concluding with the root exercise of I AM

Bibliography 191

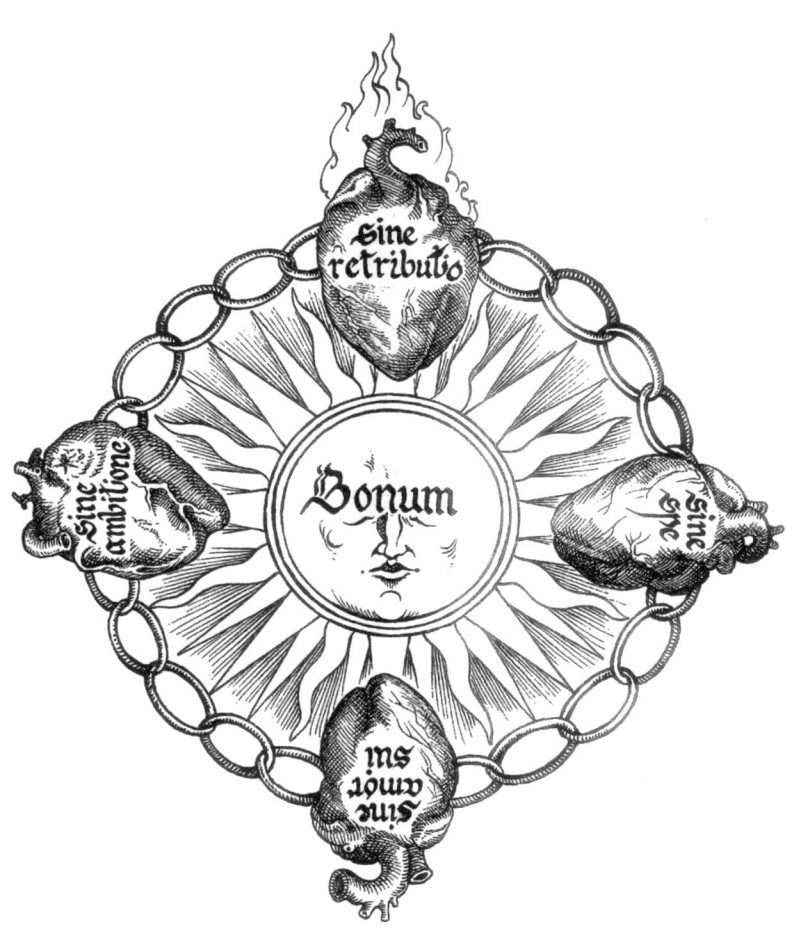

Instead of an Introduction
On the Rose and the Cross

Rosicrucian Magic. The title of this book requires explanation; first and foremost of what is meant by the very word *Rosicrucian*. And so this is where we will begin.

The term is a compound of the Latin words for rose and cross, and quickly became widespread and well known in 17th-century Europe following the publication of the three original Rosicrucian manifests, *Fama Fraternitatis*, 1614; *Confessio Fraternitatis*, 1615; and *The Chymical Wedding of Christian Rosencreutz*, 1616.

While Adam Haslmayr (c. 1560-1630) often remains overlooked as the original initiator of the purported brotherhood[1], the original three pamphlets were released in the years following the death of Tobias Hess (1568-1614), the German lawyer, Paracelsian medic and polymath from whose mystical circle they emerged. Two other close members of this circle were Christoph Besold (1577-1638) and Johann Valentin Andreae (1586-1654). Hess's ties to the multitudinous family of the Andreae are well documented, as he is already known to have practiced alchemical experiments with Johan Valentin's father.[2]

As Carlos Gilly has established, it is highly likely that all three pamphlets were written around the year 1610 with the intention of releasing them at the same time.[3] However, for unknown reasons the publication strategy never materialised, and we find further edited versions of the original manuscripts in print from 1614 onwards. At least for two of them, the *Confessio* as well as the *Chymical Wedding*, the authorship of Johan Valentin Andreae is indisputable; the exact authorship of the *Fama* still remains enigmatic, but most likely involved

---

1 see Gilly, 1994
2 Brecht, p. 34
3 Gilly, 1998, p. 12-16

Andreae as well as multiple other hands from the active circle around Tobias Hess.[4]

The allegorical nature of these original pamphlets, deliberately ambiguous and playful in their evocation of an ancient order and its founding father 'C.R.C.', has successfully remained intentionally mysterious for more than 400 years. Unsurprisingly, even today we find ourselves surrounded by a vast array of exegetical attempts to delineate their central symbol and to parse the term *rosicross*. One interpreter, the alchemist Robert Fludd (1574–1637), envisioned the sign of the rosicross as a cross sprinkled with drops of blood. French scholar Gabriel Naudé (1600–1653) revealed it as a symbol of fraternal silence and secrecy. As for the name, Eusèbe Renaudot (1646-1720) derived its meaning from the Latin word for *dew*, *ros* and a reinterpretation of the Latin word *crux* into *lux*, i.e. *light*.

Not only did these early interpreters lack the benefit of rigorous scientific debate[5], but more importantly, their symbolic constructions had rather insignificant connections to the original source texts upon which the speculations were based.[6]

Thus for the application of the term *rosicross* in the present volume I am taking a decidedly biographical approach. Following Will-Erich Peuckert's seminal study from 1928[7], the rich material that has come down to us from the life of Johann Valentin Andreae, the central author of the three pamphlets, seems the most resilient and sustainable access route to discovering more about the underlying meaning of the neologism.

Andreae's authorship of the *Chymical Wedding* has been attested to by himself, and it is within this manuscript that we find the most elaborate description of the ominous Father R.C., i.e. the famous protagonist and original namesake of the Rosicrucian Fraternity.

---

4 Gilly, 1998, p. 25; Ritman, p. 69; Brecht, pp. 65

5 Geffarth, p. 41

6 Peuckert, 1973 p. 46

7 Will-Erich Peuckert, *Das Rosenkreutz*, Berlin: Erich Schmidt Verlag, 1973 (1928)

> *Es ist nicht leicht, Gedankengänge eines Jünglings des sechzehnten Jahrhunderts, das ein recht anderes als das zwanzigste gewesen ist, verlässlich nachzugehen. Die Crux der ganzen Geschichtsschreibung war und ist ja immer die, dass man Geschehnisse älterer Zeit aus heutzutagigen interpretiert, dass man das Denken mittelalterlicher oder anderszeitiger Menschen aus den geläufigen Aussagen unserer Tage zu verstehen sucht.* [8]

•

> *It is not easy to reliably retrace the thought processes of a young man of the sixteenth century, which was quite different from the twentieth. The crux of the whole historiography was and is always, that one interprets events of an earlier time from today's vantage point, and that one tries to understand the thinking of other times from the common parlance of our own.* [9]

In a profoundly symbolic manner, the opening paragraph of the *Chymical Wedding* Andreae introduces the reader to his protagonist, the old father Christian *Rosenkreutz* (German for *Rosicross*). We encounter him as a humble hermit in his cell, living in a remote cottage, speaking regularly with God and His angels in prayer and vision.[10]

> *On an Evening before Easter-Day, I sat at a table and having (as was my custom) in my humble prayer sufficiently conversed with my Creator and considered many great mysteries [...]* [11]

The old man emerges from an intense and horrifying vision bruised but with "childlike confidence" and having received the invitation to a "Chymical Wedding". At the end of the first chapter, we find him preparing himself for the journey to the royal court and putting on his "wedding garment":

---

8 Peuckert, 1973, p. 64

9 Peuckert, 1973, p. 64

10 Peuckert, 1973, p. 48

11 Martin (ed.), p. 13

> *Hereupon I prepared myself for the way, put on my white linen coat, and girded my loins with a blood-red ribbon bound cross-ways over my shoulder. In my hat I stuck four red roses, that I might sooner by this token be taken notice of amongst the throng.*[12]

As has been observed by Peuckert, here we witness the protagonist turning into the very symbol of his name, as the ritual dress is the rosicross: A red St. Andrew's cross on white ground, formed by the ribbon looped around his shoulders, and adorned by four roses on his hat.[13] Now, we do not know if the protagonist took his name from this very dress, or whether the dress was designed to match his symbolic name. However, we do know that Johann Valentin Andreae gave us a most direct biographical clue with it. To fully recognise its importance, we have to understand more about Johann Valentin Andreae, and in particular about his grandfather Jakob Andreae (1528-1590).

As his biographer Martin Brecht observed, among the many iridescent talents we encounter in Johann Valentin Andreae, his own first and foremost passion was genealogy.[14] Sixteen years after the publication of the *Fama Fraternitas*, in 1630, Andreae published a book of very similar title: The extensive genealogy of his own family, spanning over more than five hundred pages, and released under the title *Fama Andreana Reflorescens*, with a particular focus on the larger-than-life figure of his grandfather, Jakob Andreae.

The reverence paid by Andreae to his lineage is especially noticeable, as his family origins were by no means extraordinarily ancient or otherwise distinguished. In fact they were quite the opposite: His great-grandfather Jakob Endriss had immigrated as a simple ironsmith to the Duchy of Württemberg and the city of Waiblingen. Even more significant in light of this was the rapid ascent of his son of the same name, Jakob Andreae (the new surname *Andreae* was the Latinised form of 'Son of Endriss'). The son of an ironsmith rose to become

---

12 Martin (ed.), p. 24
13 Peuckert, 1973, p. 48
14 Brecht, p. 11

a Protestant priest, a professor of theology, a general-superintendent and eventually the chancellor of the University of Tübingen. During the thirty-seven years from his appointment to professorship to his death, the territory Andreae traveled stretched from Paris to Prague and from Denmark to Bern. Jakob Andreae thus single-handedly shaped, carved and laid the cornerstones of the family's proud, yet comparatively young reputation.

Already during his funeral address in 1590 a colleague referenced him as "a man who had accompanied and decisively shaped the church history of Germany in all important matters for almost half a century"[15].

> *It is admirable how Andreae, a figure of great significance in church history, worked with the greatest dedication for the propagation and preservation of the Gospel and evangelical congregations, even in the smallest of spaces, despite the incredible abundance of his commitments. His efforts had a single centre: the preaching of the Gospel. [...] Andreae's appeal to the duty of the authorities to promote and protect the Gospel and the congregations by no means resulted in the spiritual disenchantment of the people. The sermons show to what spiritual discernment Andreae was able to educate even illiterate people like the peasants of Wachendorf with simple, accurate words. There can be no suspicion of servitude to princes in this man, who admittedly lived entirely within the political and social orders of the time. The manifold admonitions that high lords - with all due respect - heard from his mouth speak against it. In the manner of the apostle Paul, he knew that he was connected with the congregations, and nothing pained him more than their endangerment by the authorities, whether they sought to enrich themselves with church property or wavered in their faith.* [16]

After this short excursus on the man to whom Johann Valentin Andreae would feel deeply loyal and indebted for his entire life, we

---

15 Raeder, 1999

16 Raeder, 1999

can return to our biographical exploration of the symbol of the rosi-cross: In 1554 Duke Ottheinrich von der Pfalz (1502-1559) awarded Jakob Andreae the honour of their own family coat of arms.

The coat of arms of Paracelus, Luther and Andreae,
source: Peuckert, 1973, p. 60

In its centre it shows a red St. Andrew's cross with one of four red roses in each quadrant. In the later self-staging of his own portraits, Johann Valentin Andreae would take great care to include this coat of arms, as well as in some cases additional fictitious ones.[17]

However, as we learn from Andreae's own writings, the spirit from which such ancestral references were born was not at all one of noble entitlement. Quite the opposite: Through his own works, we begin to understand Johann Valentin Andreae as a man who recognised the burdensome legacy he had inherited from his benefactors. He knew none of it was of any value by lineage of blood or initiation alone. At best these could act as reminders of the sincere obligation he had to follow the examples of the ones who had come before him. His charge was to bring their virtues to life, to resurrect them within himself, and to manifest their ideals in his own words and deeds.

> *(540.) Lächerlich ist der Adel, wenn er sich sich bei Tisch zuprostend der Tugend und Tapferkeit seiner Ahnen rühmt, es sei denn, er selber sei von grosser Tapferkeit und Tugend, nach dem Motto: mein Stammbaum beginne bei mir selbst!* [18]

---

17 Brecht, p. 13

18 Johann Valentin Andreae, Theca Gladii Spiritus, p. 189

(540.) The nobility is ridiculous when it boasts of the virtue and bravery of its ancestors at table, unless it itself is of great bravery and virtue, according to the motto: my family tree begins with myself! [19]

Thus, in the allegorical father figure of *Christian Rosencreutz* we encounter Johann Valentin Andreae himself, standing in the reverent shadow of the men who shaped him, chief among these his grandfather Jakob Andreae and his spiritual mentor Tobias Hess.

Contemporary portrait of Jakob Andraeae,
source: Landeskirchliches Archiv Stuttgart, Bildersammlung, Nr. 2534

---

19 Johann Valentin Andreae, Theca Gladii Spiritus, p. 189

Following the lead of these two eminent men, we discover two further clues unlocking the intent with which Johan Valentin Andreae would begin using the symbol of the rosicross

A contemporary portrait from the time of Jakob Andreae's death in 1590 shows the grandfather framed in a classical cartridge-oval and surrounded by five emblematic Latin mottoes.

- Top left, shows an anchor: *Fuit Huic Spes anchora Vitae. To this one hope was an anchor.*
- Top centre, shows a fiery heart with the name Jesus written upon it: *Nil hoc Felicius Igne. Nothing is more auspicious than this fire.*
- Top right, shows a rose growing from thorns: *Sic patientia Crevit. In this way forbearance grows.*
- Bottom right, shows a candle upon a book: *Alijs Servire paratus. Ready to serve others.*
- Bottom left, shows a skull with crown ring from which grow ears of corn: *Mortem Honor iste secutus. Thus honour followed death.*

About fifteen to twenty years before Johan Valentin Andreae is believed to have written his Rosicrucian manuscripts, we find explicit interpretation of the symbol of the rose in their family tradition. Amongst the four unconditional qualities of piety (anchor), humbleness (skull) and service (flame), the rose represented patience, forbearance or longanimity, as the Latin word patientia can be translated as all three English words. Specifically, the rose blossom symbolises this quality not as a rigidly enforced virtue, but as an organically grown attitude paradoxically emerging from thorns. The rose is brought to life by the thorn bush, i.e. it cannot be attained unless one is lovingly willing to live deeply invested in a flawed, cruel and tantalising world.

By way of comparison to Johann Valentin Andreae's 1616 *Theca Gladii Spiritus* (Latin for *Scabbard of the Spiritual Sword*), we discover that the symbolism of the thorns from which the rose of forbearance emerges matches exactly the author's classic use of another crucial Christian symbol: the cross. In harmony with the fourteen classical Stations of the Cross, we find the cross mentioned in precisely fourteen of the eight-hundred aphorisms of the book. Johann Valentin Andreae originally published the Theca as eight-hundred pronouncements of his teacher Tobias Hess. However, as Martin Brecht was able to demonstrate, they emerged directly from the quill of our author, even containing several direct quotes of the Confessio. This work is believed to haver been written at the same time as the Rosicrucian documents, under the strong influence of the mystical circle that had formed around the polymath Tobias Hess.[20]

Let's read a few of the aphorisms relating to the nature of the cross according to Johann Valentin Andreae. The aphorisms help us understand the cross's paradoxical nature, in which suffering and grace are bound into one. The aphorisms will also reveal an explicitly anti-Gnostic stance, for according to Andreae, redemption from the world is not to be gained by withdrawal from a world of suffering, but by fully immersing oneself into the life meant for us to live. The stated mystical goal was to be in this world and yet not from this world, to be present within it without commingling with its raw and animalistic qualities.

> *(71.) Unser Kreuz muss das sein, das Gott uns als Kreuz sendet, und dies verletzt uns dort, wo wir verwundbar sind. Er passt nämlich jedem sein eigenes Kreuz an, damit jeder seufzt und keiner unter seinem Kreuz zu lachen vermag.*

> *(95.) Wessen Leib unter dem Kreuz altert, dessen Seele verjüngt sich für Gott.*

> *(210.) Mit dem Kreuz versehen, wandeln wir nicht mehr blind vor so vielen Zeichen Gottes durch diese Welt, sondern erkennen die Ursache für ein Geschehen, das die anderen törichterweise für blossen Zufall halten.*

> *(277.) Für die Seinen ist Gott am Kreuz ein Wunder.*

---

20 Gilly, 1998, p. 25

(501.) Das Leben Christi sei wie ein Schiff für den Christen, dessen Mastbaum das Kreuz, das Segel das Zeichen des herrlichen Siegs Christi, der Leitstern der Glaube, die Ruder Gebete, Nächstenliebe, Geduld und Mäßigung, die Verpflegung das Wort Gottes, der Mantel die Unschuld Christi, der Anker der göttliche Wille, die Winde das Wehen des Heiligen Geistes; so ausgerüstet wird er bald am Gestade der christlichen Einfalt in den langersehnten Hafen des ewigen Erbes einlaufen.

(631.) Das Reich Christi triumphiert eher durch das Kreuz als durch Macht und Reichtum; je tapferer es hier duldet, desto heller wird es ein strahlen.

(734.) Zum rechten Leben sind allein als Hilfsmittel noch übrig: die Rechtschaffenheit der Eltern, günstige Zeit- und Ortsumstände, fleissige Unterweisung durch gewissenhafte Erzieher, fromme Gebete, Vermeidung der Gelegenheit zur Sünde, rastlose Arbeit, Lebenserfahrung, vor allem aber die Einübung ins Tragen des Kreuzes; nur dies alles kann den Überfluss unserer Bosheit vernichten und uns endlich, wenn auch widerwillig, zur Einsicht bringen.

•

(71.) Our cross must be the one that God sends us as a cross, and this hurts us where we are vulnerable. Indeed, he adapts to everyone their own cross, so that everyone sighs and no one is able to laugh under his cross.

(95.) Whose body ages under the cross, his soul rejuvenates for God.

(210.) Provided with the cross, we no longer walk blindly before so many signs of God through this world, but recognize the cause of an event, which the others foolishly believe to be mere coincidence.

(277.) For the ones who follow him, God on the cross is a miracle.

(501.) Let the life of Christ be like a ship for the Christian, whose mast is the cross, the sail the sign of Christ's glorious victory, the guiding star faith, the oars prayers, charity, patience, and temperance,

> the victual the word of God, the mantle the innocence of Christ, the anchor the divine will, the winds the blowing of the Holy Spirit; thus equipped he will soon sail on the shore of Christian simplicity into the long-awaited harbor of the eternal inheritance.
>
> *(631.)* The kingdom of Christ triumphs rather by the cross than by power and wealth; the more valiantly it endures here, the brighter it will shine.
>
> *(734.)* For the right life there remain only these aids: the righteousness of parents, favorable circumstances of time and place, diligent instruction by conscientious educators, pious prayers, avoidance of the occasion of sin, restless labor, experience of life, but above all training in the bearing of the cross; only all this can destroy the abundance of our wickedness and bring us at last, though reluctantly, to understanding.

When studying the Theca in its paradoxical entirety, we discover a Hermetic-magical worldview overtly inspired by the writings of Joachim of Fiore (1135–1202), Johannes Trithemius (1462–1516), Paracelsus (1494–1541) and Jakob Böhme (1575–1624), yet superimposed with the deeply Protestant everyday ethics that Johann Valentin Andreae inherited from his grandfather. In fact, the Theca reveals many keys to the allegorical riddles presented in the original Rosicrucian manifests, especially when it comes to the actual nature of this alleged fraternity. Thus, unsurprisingly, we find another such key when relating the symbol of the cross to the single aphorism that makes mention of the rose:

> *(241.) Durch Gestrüpp und Dornen muss man sich zu dem Garten durchkämpfen, wo die weissen und blutroten Rosen blühen.*
>
> •
>
> *(241.)* Through brushwood and thorns one must fight one's way to the garden where the white and blood-red roses bloom.

The *cross* and the *thorns* are symbols neither of vain nor random suffering, but of a divine path for the wise. In the context of the *Theca* the idea of *bearing one's cross* should not be misread as an expression of purely masochistic Medieval *Leidensmystik*. Rather it addresses each one of us in our human individuality, encouraging us to realise loss, hardship and plight not as an unnecessary burden in an otherwise hedonistic life, but as the path of personal growth that Divinity has prepared for us.

When we now place the symbol of the rose into the middle of this cross of the world, we arrive at the dual meaning of the white and blood-red roses: The red rose symbolises the above mentioned virtue of forbearance and longanimity, the gentleness we are encouraged to bring both to ourselves as well as to the flawed world we live in.

The white rose, on the other hand, symbolises the mystical secret, the divine plant, surrounded by silence, which cannot be taken from the Hermetic rose garden where only the wise will find it. By calling out these two different coloured roses, Johann Valentin Andreae reminds his readers of the virtues we are to display towards the world and the silence of the adept leading into the inner secrets of their mystical journey, respectively. Finally, by placing them in the mystical rose garden, Andreae may be giving us an echo of the Paracelsian mago-alchemical instructions of the same title:

> *So will ich dir schenken die folgenden Stücklein zu vernehmen die weissen Rosen, auf dass die wahrhaftige Lehre daraus komme. [...]*
>
> *Also siehst du, mein lieber Freund, wie viel guter Stück und Kunst dir angezeigt in diesem meinem Rosengarten. Aber jedoch kannst du durch solchen Weg nichts ausrichten, damit du Rosen aus diesem Garten bringest. Denn er ist ja wohl bewahret mit tiefem Graben, starken Mauern, festen Pfosten und also verwahret, dass kein Mensch darein kommen kann, er gehe denn durch die 7 Pforten der Metalle ein, denn er ist mit Riegeln wohl verschlossen.*
>
> *Ein schönes Gebet: 'O liebster, gütigster, barmherziger Gott, so ich hier in etwas gesündigt habe, so siehe auf mich mit deinen gnädigen und gütigen Augen, denn du bist allein der Brunnen und Grund der Barmherzigkeit. Und bitte dich ganz demütig, du wolltest mich Weisheit und Verstand lehren, dass allein mein getreuer Gärtner, der*

> *Heilige Geist, mich erleuchte und erfülle, dass ich den Schlüssel zu dem Rosengarten finde, damit ich ihn aufschliessen kann und möge.'²¹*

•

> *So I will give you the following little pieces to hear the white roses, so that the true teaching may come from them. [...]*
>
> *So you see, my dear friend, how many good pieces and art are shown to you in this rose garden of mine. But by such means you can do nothing to bring roses out of this garden. For it is well guarded with a deep moat, strong walls, solid posts and so guarded that no man can enter it, unless he enters through the 7 gates of metals, for it is well locked with bolts.*
>
> *A beautiful prayer: 'O most loving, kind, merciful God, if I have sinned here in anything, look upon me with your gracious and kind eyes, for you alone are the fountain and ground of mercy. And most humbly beseech thee, that thou wouldst teach me wisdom and understanding, that my faithful gardener alone, the Holy Spirit, may enlighten and fill me, that I may find the key to the rose garden, that I may be able and will unlock it.'* ²²

Much more could be said about the *rosicross* and its deep roots in Johann Valentin Andreae's biography. How it was his teacher's teacher, Simon Studion (1543-1608) who first depicted it in an extensive numerological study inspired through angelic contact, the *Naometria*; how Andreae later in his life rejected chiliastic speculation as well as astrology but reaffirmed magic according to a pansophic ideal. In this pater phase of his beliefs, Andrea advocated for a spiritual community of the like-minded that would focus on living benefaction, education and healing for the poor.

However, for the purpose of this introduction, we will confine ourselves to examining a few seminal aphorisms from the scabbard that holds the spiritual sword:

---

21 Paracelsus, in: Spunda (ed.), p. 43
22 Paracelsus, in: Spunda (ed.), p. 43

(10.) Ob wir es wollen oder nicht: manches, was zum Lernstoff gehört, müssen wir lernen.

(33.) Der soll schweigen, der Mysterien nicht erfunden hat, sondern dem sie nur berichtet wurden.

(78.) Summer aller Gebete und vollendetes Glück: Gott ähnlich zu werden.

(87.) Erbitte von Gott nicht, dass Seine Medizin dir schmecke, sondern dass sie dir helfe.

(88.) Was ist Christentum? Die Ähnlichkeit mit Gott, soweit der menschlichen Natur möglich. Hast du dich entschlossen Christ zu sein, so eile ihm ähnlich zu werden, bekleide dich mit Christus.

(105.) Lehren: durch sittliches Vorbild oder gar nicht!

(106.) Das wollen wir lernen: weise zu urteilen, glücklich zu leben und der Welt nicht zu dienen.

(107.) Der höchste Lenker verleiht den Demütigen Ansehen, stößt die Hochmütigen in quälende Finsternis, sendet den Schweigsamen die Engel zur Unterredung und schickt die Schwätzer in die Wüste.

(108.) Magier wird genannt, wer es vermag, die grossen Buchstaben, doe Gott dem Weltgebäude einschrieb und mit der Abfolge der Reiche mehrmals wiederholte, zu lesen und daraus belehrt zu werden.

(296.) Es ist nicht so leicht, wie manche glauben, Menschen zu beherrschen, und noch dazu solche von sehr freier Sinnesart; manchmal muss man die Augen zudrücken und warten bis sie sich ausgetobt haben.

(326.) Anfang und Ende liegen im Kreis sehr eng beieinander.

(557.) Magie ist das – fleissige – Studium vieler Künste.

(799.) Schwer gibt man alte Gewohnheiten auf: niemand lässt sich gern über das hinausführen, was er sehen kann.

(800.) Wissenschaft bläht auf, Liebe nützt anderen.

(10.) Whether we like it or not: some things, which belong to the curriculum, we have to learn.

(33.) Let him be silent, who did not invent mysteries, but to whom they were only reported.

(78.) Sum of all prayers and perfect happiness: to become like God.

(87.) Do not ask God to make His medicine taste good to you, but to help you.

(88.) What is Christianity? The alikeness to God, as far as possible to human nature. If you have decided to be a Christian, hurry to become alike to Him, clothe yourself with Christ.

(105.) Teaching: Through virtuous example, or not at all.

(106.) This is what we want to learn: to judge wisely, to live happily, and not to serve the world.

(107.) The supreme guide gives prestige to the humble, pushes the haughty into tormenting darkness, sends the silent the angels for conversation and sends the talkers into the desert.

(108) He is called a magician who is able to read and to be instructed by the great letters which God inscribed in the building of the world and repeated several times with the succession of the kingdoms.

(296) It is not so easy as some believe to lead people, and even more so those of a very free nature; sometimes one has to close one's eyes and wait until they have run riot.

(326.) Beginning and end are very close together in the circle.

(557.) Magic is the - diligent - study of many arts.

(799.) It is difficult to give up old habits: nobody likes to be led beyond what they can see.

(800.) Science inflates, love benefits others.

Hopefully what we remember from these short elucidations on the nature of the rose and the cross, or the *rosicross* according to the biographical echo of Johann Valentin Andreae, is not at all about any kind of occult orthodoxy or clinging literally to the words of one's predecessor. Otherwise Andreae would have never allowed himself to turn away from the complex cabalistic speculations of Simon Studion where he first encountered the rose in the centre of the cross (see original illustrations on the following double page). Rather, the *rosicross* of the author and editor of the first Rosicrucian manifests symbolised a genuine mystical way of life.

A way, that is, which leads out of the Gnostics's escapism and convoluted eschatology, back into the world of creation, with the calm intent to quietly withstand its storms, to hear the Lion before Midnight roar, while standing in man's intended place: One's feet anchored deep in the abyss, head on heaven's horizon, heart open and illuminated, hands ready to serve.

Rosicrucian Magic, therefore, is the kind of magic that enables and illuminates our path towards heightened presence in the world; perhaps not yet fully alike to Divinity, but certainly on the narrow trail to becoming alike to the angelic mind.

nothing is more auspicious than this fire

Hope is the anchor of life

Forbearance grows like a rose

When the storms arrive

I will be safe and poised.

Head above the horizon. Feet anchored in the Abyss.

Body engulfed in flames. Heart among the roses.

All these tempests may come

As I was made to bear this cross.

Lo! Storm from the North, come and blow!

Lo! Lion before midnight, approach and roar!

For I am a flame to withstand storms

And you are a rose to stand with me.

Holy. Holy. Holy.

Honor follows death

Ready to serve others

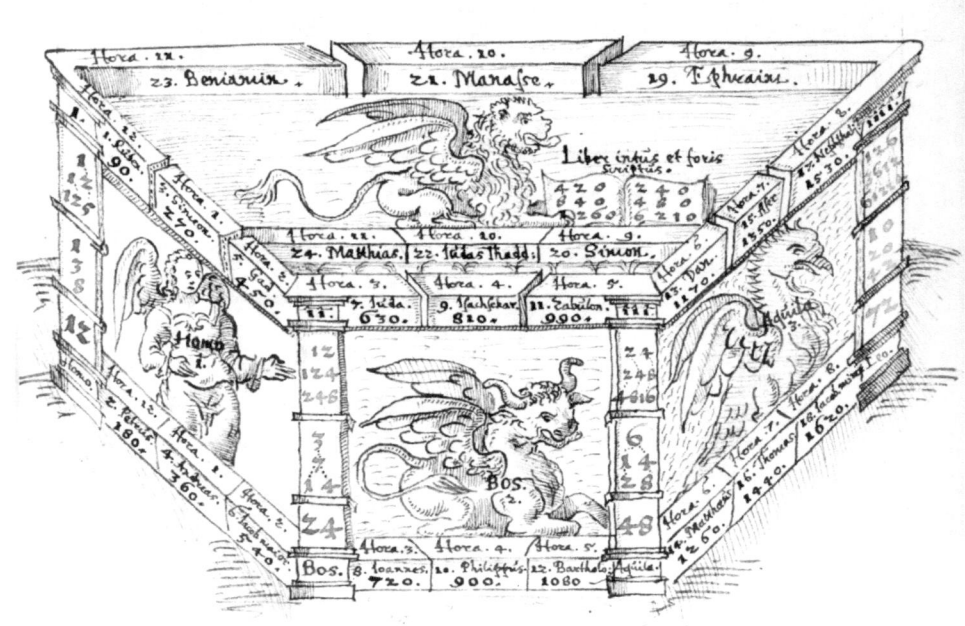

Stimon Studion's depiction of the side view of the city of Jericho,
guarded by the four beings of the quarters,
source: *Naometria, Teil 1*, s.l., 1604, p. 11

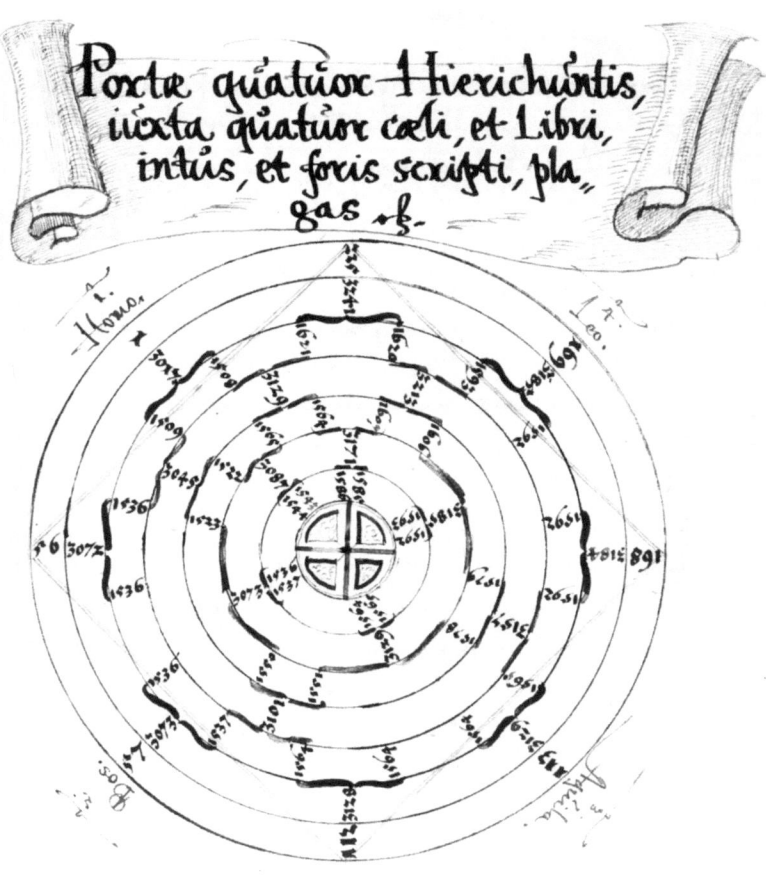

Stimon Studion's first depiction of the rose in the centre of
the cross as the top view of the spiritual city of Jericho,
source: *Naometria, Teil 1*, s.l., 1604, p. 271

Chapter 1.

Entering the Temple. Entering the World.

White magic. The term is so overused and yet ill-defined. The three books of the Holy Daimon cycle I published with Scarlet Imprint from 2018 to 2021 focussed on excavating white magic's diverse historic origins and practices. And as I have come to understand in hindsight, my personal practice and study over the last fifteen years centered upon restoring and reactivating a magical current that is best summarised under this term. So it seems an opportune moment to sharpen the saw on how I am using it.

Carlos Gilly famously called the *Arbatel* the first book of white magic.[1] That of course is a rather theoretical claim. For as we know, nothing in magic appears out of nowhere and most things have been discovered before, only to be slowly swallowed again by the rolling tides of time. Many works of magic have paved the way to the expression of white magic as we encounter it in the Arbatel. And yet, Carlos Gilly is correct that few if any of these had been printed before. Thus, we can agree that the Arbatel can fairly claim to be the first printed book on white magic.

The relatively unknown series of manuscripts that had preceded the Arbatel only by a few decades – a series essential to the form of magic we encounter in the latter – were the writings of a cryptic author named *Pelagius the Hermit*. We explore these manuscripts and their close entanglement with the figure of Johannes Trithemius in *Black Abbot · White Magic*.[2] In the follow-up book *Holy Heretics*[3] we undertake a tour de force over almost two millennia, tracing many

---

1 Gilly, 2002
2 Frater Acher, 2020
3 Frater Acher, 2021

of the practical origins of white magic, their detours and dead ends as well as their shortcuts and forgotten gems; all of which ultimately coalesced in the Late Medieval period in a rejuvenated viewpoint of man's position and purpose in Nature. We conclude the Holy Daimon cycle at the end of *Holy Heretics* with a fully restored ritual which mends the fragmentary nature of the Arbatel and allows practitioners to initiate themselves into the current of magic we jointly rediscovered.

It is obvious from the above that whenever I use the term *white magic* I am standing knee-deep in the magical currents that reemerged in early 16th century Germany. A practitioner of this current would have considered themselves as much a mystic and divine servant, as they would have thought of themselves as hard-working everyday folk. They would aim to stand with one foot in the cloud of unknowing and with the other in either the field, the workshop, or the circle of art.

However, to offer a broad-brush profile of this current of magic it might be best to contrast it with what it never was nor attempted to be. To that effect only, we could contrast black and white magic according to the following qualities. What is critical to embrace though, is that neither of these terms contain an ethical or values-based judgement.

In their essence, both terms relate to the non-colours of black and white and their specific qualities: For black to absorb all light in its centre, and for white to reflect all of it back into its circumference. Equally, in actual practice they are not meant to be mutually exclusive, but rather symbiotic.

You see, no one lives life with hands open all the time. The beauty of life is following its tides: Opening and closing our hands, breathing in and out, taking and giving. The imbalance in Western magic, in my humble opinion, is that at least since the early Middle Ages our current had turned into a (literary) tradition that was all about closing one's hand.

	Black Magic	White Magic
Symbol	Closed Hand	Open Hand
Focussed	On a Gain	On an Encounter
Goal	Changing Circumstances	Changing Consciousness
Foundation	Based upon Control by the Operator	Based upon Grace by Divinity
Technique	Drawing the Spirit into the Operator's Realm	Aligning the Operator's Spirit to the Spirit's Realm
Direction	Flows into the Circle	Flows out into the World
Central Risk	Controlling Cause-Effect Correlation	Controlling Exposure and Obscuration
Begins with	The Hand	The Heart-Flame
Essential tool	**The Evocation**	**The Prayer**
Operator's role	The Rod	The Gate

Western Magic had devolved into a substitute pathway towards power acquisition and economic growth. That is why until this day every narcissistic soul who believes life owes them, feels so at home in the genre of the Medieval Grimoires. For centuries Western Magic has turned into the spiritual equivalent of the Crusades or the Spanish

Reconquista: A feeble attempt to claim their sure birth right, failing to realise that what lies behind such spiritual warfare is merely ignorance and the essential inability to understand and appreciate otherness.

This is what *white magic* could become to us again: A cure, a re-balancing of the poison, a necessary lent and diet from the constant craving of power that has become synonymous with our Western Tradition of Magic. It is a return to work in true partnership. And for that it takes a lot of preparation. Not (only) in technical skill gains, but much more essentially in preparing and drawing out again the pure light of our heart-flame. We have to turn ourselves from the rod that aims to direct the world as a donkey (our brains), into the gate that is open to channel the tide without breaking itself. What a marvellous goal and journey! And we shall keep humbleness at our side at all times.

For that is what white magic is about at its heart: The humility to realise that the vessel our human spirits have been poured into at birth, is one of the smallest containers in the spirit world. Our part of the weave is tiny. And true, we humans are tiny spirits, and yet mighty in our versatility. If you like, humans are the Swiss Army knives of spirit vessels: We are the personified unintentional utility, among a world that is born from divine purpose. We are the best at inserting ourselves into any crack and fissure of creation, and breaking it apart for good. This we do without really knowing why, like a child feverishly excited when witnessing its impact on the world. But different from a child, we gain the tools and qualities of a magician only as an adult.

White magic, therefore, is all about owning our fair share. It is about going slow, very slow indeed. Only in this way do we realise how much power we can unfold with each step, if only placed with true divine intent.

So, what does this mean on a more practical personal level? Let's begin with the most obvious point.

Integrity, some say, is what you do when nobody is watching. And God, others say, is always watching. Yet neither of these statements, from a magician's perspective, is hitting the mark. A fire has no centre and no periphery. A sea's heart is everywhere and nowhere at once. The entire being of a storm is embedded in each gust. A storm is no more or less storm in the squall that touches you or any one else.

In the same manner, I suggest, a magician should think of themselves: Not as a being installed in skin, but as a cloud of consciousness, expressing all of itself in each act. Whether we grant significance to this act or not is entirely irrelevant. For the significance that matters resides beyond the sphere of the living. It is a different place altogether. It is a place where our biggest decisions are equal to our smallest, where each mortal's step matters, and simultaneously doesn't, where fates are woven by a glance and a cue, and yet the weaving continues eternally.

On this level, we humans too are a natural force. Each one of us is a tiny portion of it. And this natural force called *humanness* can only be experienced when it encounters the rest of the world, Malkuth.

Now, what determines this force's quality and nature is entirely up to us. And that is why this force is so magical and unique; it carries a seed nothing else in Malkuth was granted, the seed of free will. And the only way to experience this force that we are, and this seed that we were given, is as a human applying themselves against the world.

Free will is nothing at all – unless we awaken it, by holding ourselves up against the world. It is in the contact between each human and the world, that the game the gods began so long ago will end. As we will see in a later chapter, the old Kabbalists had a word for this idea; they called it *tikkune*.

How we hold ourselves is everything – not because God is watching, but because there is nothing else that we are. We are empty within, just like fire, oceans and storms are empty from within. There is nothing other to them than being fire, being oceans and being storms. Each of their expressions, each time we encounter them, are perfectly expressed. And so it is with us humans.

Our way of being, our way of seeing, the way we decide to hold ourselves towards the world is all we have. All of our acts flow through the prism of our presence. Each breath. Each step. There is no way around it.

For a magician this should not come as a surprise. For isn't this how we came to think of the spirits – of storm demons and chthonic sleepers, of hive-beings and angelic structures? None of them are mounted in skin. All of them seem as fleeting as free. They can come and go, apply themselves against the world and withdraw from it, like a magical tide. All their myths and personas over centuries were not made up by who they are within, by what they were born from, or what they strive towards – but instead by how they behave towards the world. Each being, be it angelic, human or otherwise, is defined by its encounter with the world. Without it, we are nothing but potential enshrined. The world is the divination bowl, filled with black waters, into which the gods stare, and see us.

Johannes Trithemius believed evil angels were God's way of testing our free will. According to him, demons held no agency in themselves, that is unless we granted them access to the seed that was given to us: Free will.[4]

Integrity according to such a worldview is nothing we strive to achieve for God or others. It is not at all a social good. But it is the most essential of all magical capabilities: To let each of our decisions count, as if we were standing in front of the scales of *Ma'at*. And yet not to become self-judging or orthodox, but to stay connected to the flowing tides of life, like fire does. What an exquisite challenge.

White magic, as we might want to rediscover it together, is exceptional in so far as it focusses mainly on how we apply our free will towards the world. It teaches the handling of magic as a force, not for escaping, but for pulling closer into the world.

---

4 Brann, 1999, p.41

And yet white magic might be more mystical in its experience and impact than the lives of many self-proclaimed hermits ever were. Because it strips away anything unnecessary, and holds us grounded in, exposed to everyday life.

Like any good mystical path, it appears Saturnian towards the world, and is unconditional in its demand towards how we show up in the world.

Speaking Ma'at.
Doing Ma'at.

This is not a book about Egyptian Magic. Neither do we intend to retrace the actual historic influences of Egyptian Magic on the magic of the Western Late Middle Ages. And still, we will benefit from looking into the mirror which is Ma'at. If we decide to do so – only a few pages into this slender book, introducing a historic inconsistency that might seem unnecessary – then it is with the sole intent to knock us slightly off-centre.

This book is written from the viewpoint and with the experience of the animistic spirit-practitioner, and yet we aim to be historically accurate in our attempt to retrace some influences which shaped what we like to call Rosicrucian Magic.

Several times over the course of this text we will switch mental frameworks – and step from the academic sphere into the one of living magic. Obviously, they both exist simultaneously while following very different rules; and any serious attempt to write about magic has to balance on the threshold of the two. Crossing this threshold backwards and forwards in a single text holds the risk of confusing the reader, yet it also holds the potential to loosen mental frameworks. By exposing ourselves to a healthy dose of cognitive dissonance we will automatically get out of the step of our usual ways of making sense of the world.

Looking into the mirror of Ma'at matters little in regard to the historic explorations of the manuscripts we will examine in this text. If this is your only interest, feel free to skip this current chapter. Understanding Ma'at matters deeply though through the lens of the practicing magician: From that vantage point Ma'at is entirely agnostic in regards to any cultural or historic influences. The magical fulcrum which is Ma'at simply is.

Ancient Egyptians long ago gave it the name *Ma'at*; yet it existed namelessly for aeons before. Looking into its mirror matters deeply with regards what we'd love for the reader to do with the magic contained on these pages, once they get to the end of this small book. For upholding the balance of Ma'at is one of the highest goals an adept can aspire to. It is also the exact spirit and intent from which the Rosicrucian world-reformation was born (or rather rediscovered).

And yet, only the practicing magician is allowed to make the latter statement. For the 21st-century publishing academic it would equal suicide. Which is why we'd like for our readers to loosen the mental framework that distinguishes these two ways of looking at one world, the one we live in neither as magicians nor academics, but as full human beings.

With this in mind, we will dare to offer an unconditional glance at the mirror that has come to be known as Ma'at.

•

If our eyes allowed us to see the inner dynamics of a human body, we would quickly overcome a number of misperceptions. Chief among these is the erroneous assumption that somehow by magic this compound of myriad living forces exists in a state of constant harmony. It only seems that way to us because our human senses (under normal conditions) do not perceive its ever-lasting struggle and effort.

The opposite is true though: Our bodies are constantly at work on the inside. Sometimes this work is heavy lifting, to pull us back from brink of illness, to swing an organ back into its proper rhythm when it was lost; but always it is a careful awareness, a watching and tending, a rebalancing and rearranging.

No ecosystem can maintain itself without daily struggles, and neither can our human bodies. That is why we need ample amounts of sleep, water, nutrition and sunlight — because natural resources are constantly consumed and applied. The myth of a perpetuum mobile, of a self-sustaining ecosystem, is precisely that, wishful thinking.

Real life living systems are progressively dependent on the watchful care of all their combined hive-components. A single one of them goes down, the entire system may ultimately falter.

If we aim to understand the (social) nature of Ma'at, we have to understand not only the physical planet we live on, but the entire cosmos we are woven into, as one gigantic living system. According to the Ancient Egyptians, this cosmic body follows precisely the same dynamics as any living form: It is entirely dependent on the active agency of its components to save itself from falling into chaos and disintegration. The cosmos needs care. It doesn't need a human hand alone – it needs the hands of all its visible and invisible species united in daily acts of service, integration and rejuvenation.

The term Ma'at in this context refers to much more than its often traditional translation *world-order*. It refers to the process in which the individual being or force not only realises itself, but simultaneously takes its proper place towards everything else that exists in creation. Ma'at describes the process of self-realisation just as much as self-localisation within a single hive-cosmos, where each part is attempting to speak and do Ma'at in every single movement.[5]

Let's pause for a moment and reflect on how such a worldview might differ from ours today? In a world where humans have failed so significantly to take their proper place, where a single species has almost managed to push an entire cosmos off balance, it is easy to believe that the complete extinction of this species equals healing, or *doing Ma'at*.

The Ancient Egyptians would have seen this quite differently: The simple abandoning of a habitat by an entire species, whether that is a small pond, a nature reserve, or an entire planet, will not bring it back to wholeness. While it might allow it to recover from its immediate imbalance. However, eventually, what is required for a healthy

---

5 For further reference: Assmann, 2006, or more specifically *The ethics and code of Quareia: Ma'at*, in: Josephine McCarthy, 2018

ecosystem to sustain itself, to be truly resilient to the attacking forces of chaos, is the united services of all species that were born from it — including the human one.

Ultimately, this reveals an ethical dilemma: Our human actions easily distort an ecosystem way beyond their intended consequences; yet according to Ancient Egyptian views, not acting at all is equally unethical. Doing Ma'at, as we begin to see, requires mastery just like any other learned skill. In fact, doing Ma'at is the ultimate human skill worth living for.

> *The Egyptian Gods not only were in the world, but they were the world. Their collaboration brought forth the world, i.e. the continuous process which we call 'cosmos'. To this end it required Ma'at. It ensured the synergy of all coaction, which allowed the cosmos to emerge from the constant interaction of forces and from the overcoming of opposing energies.*[6]

As we can see, in its ephemeral yet constantly rejuvenating way of being this Ancient Egyptian cosmos could not have been more different from the Ancient Greek and Gnostic ones: Nothing in the Egyptian cosmos is static, immutable, eternal and ideal; yet everything is fluid, social, changing, interdependent and organic. If the perfected form of the Greek cosmos is a flawless statue carved from white marble, the Egyptian's is the meandering, ever-breeding delta of the Nile.

•

So, what did this mean for Ancient Egyptian everyday life? Clearly Ma'at was not an abstract parameter or concept; instead it was the horizon of success for all things mundane as well as divine. How should you live? How should you love? How should you serve and rule? How should you be remembered? And how should you live on? *Speaking Ma'at, doing Ma'at* was the answer to life (and the afterlife) in all its myriad facets and dimensions. Nothing illustrates this better than the three core vices against the Ma'at: *Inertia, deafness* and *greed*.

---

6 Assmann, 2006, p. 36, translation by author

Inertia in this context was a function of forgetfulness. The sloth lived in the present moment, with no yesterday and no tomorrow. Yet without the respect for time there was no Ma'at. Every yesterday's act required a response today. Every act performed today held the promise of an echo returning tomorrow.

Ma'at was encapsulated in the demand that yesterday held for today and it required memory and active recalling. The Egyptian language had a wonderful way of expressing this idea: In the old texts we often encounter the idea that every *act* requires *joining*. Just like bricks stacked up and waiting to turn into a building, they will come to nothing, unless each deed is followed by an act of joining – a response that completes the act, provides its echo and concludes its gestalt.

It was in light of this that inertia and forgetfulness meant to untie the ribbon between act and rightful echo.

> *Acting in solidarity requires social memory, i.e. a motivational horizon that does not always constitute itself anew from day to day according to the respective interests, but goes back to the past, encompasses yesterday and today, and ties today to yesterday. This means responsible action in the sense of Ma'at.*[7]

Deafness. An Egyptian saying goes *Whoever is deaf to the Ma'at, has no friends.*[8] Just like good memory wove yesterday's acts into today, so the ability to listen wove mutual acts together into friendship and into solidarity. Acting in this context always formed a function of communication, of responding to what one had heard.

Because the Egyptian cosmos was embalmed in a process of constant birth and death, there were very few hard and fast rules. Philosophical paradigms and static maxims didn't bode well when the entire world could change overnight. What took their place instead, was everyone's ability to listen and to understand by themselves. *Speaking Ma'at and doing Ma'at* firstly requires the ability to listen.

---

7 Assmann, 2006, p. 62

8 Assmann, 2006, p. 69

It is characteristic of Egyptian language that emotions do not emerge from within the body of the perceiver but that they are thought to radiate out from the person who evokes them. Thus, it is a person (or a spirit, god, etc.) who radiates fear, love, etc, and the person next to them is simply absorbing and echoing the impulse they set free.

Exuding love – and being loved in return – thus turns into a responsibility of every single community member. This was especially so in a society where wellbeing and salvation were so closely tied to the way how one was remembered by fellow humans, spirits and progeny.

Therefore, the corresponding virtue to deafness was not simply the ability to listen, but actually the quality of one's *heart's-patience* (*Herzensgeduld*). The act of active, mindful listening depended upon one's heart's ability to be patient and to fully absorb the speaker's words. Most forms of social injustice therefore were either blamed on the disintegration of inverse acts (i.e. weaving together yesterday and today) or on one's inability to skilfully listen.

> *When what is heard enters the hearer,*
> *the hearer becomes one with the heard.*[9]

𝕲𝖗𝖊𝖊𝖉. The third and most obvious among the vices was greed. Simply put, greed was considered the anti-principle of all things Ma'at.

If Ma'at was understood as a socially positive principle, one that created synergy and coherence on the three layers of time, society and individual, then greed was its destructive, evil twin on all three layers. Greed in this context was a direct function of autarky – of placing one's personal autonomy over the common good.

---

9 Egyptian saying, originally by Amenemope: *"Give thine ear, and hear what I say, And apply thine heart to apprehend; It is good for thee to place them in thine heart, let them rest in the casket of thy belly; That they may act as a peg upon thy tongue."* (Glanville, 1942, p. 246–248)

What is important to reconcile in light of this, is that according to the Ancient Egyptian worldview all social bonds and even ties of blood depended completely on whether one managed to do Ma'at. A father or mother who did not treat their children well or failed to ensure their inheritance had no hope for prayers and requiems to be read at their grave. Being ill remembered or forgotten was the most devastating, terrifying prospect Egyptians could imagine.

Every deed, one's entire life was aimed at earning good memory among fellow citizens, family and progeny – at becoming a person who radiated love both in this life and in the afterlife.

Ma'at was the conscious antipole to a raw everyday reality that often turned out to be cruel, unfair or favouring the healthy and strong: *To speak Ma'at, to do Ma'at* precisely was not any kind of natural law, but a service that had to be chosen in every single word and act. A service directed towards realising oneself, one's community and the world one aimed to be positively woven into one with.

A man's paradise is his good nature.[10]

•

Considering these foundations of ethical conduct according to the Ancient Egyptians can act as a stark reminder to us not to attempt anything in magic that we haven't yet mastered in our mundane, everyday life. Who are we to approach chthonic or celestial spirits with the request to walk through their gates, if we can't even yet calm our hearts, and bed them on patience?

If we followed the logic of doing Ma'at we'd come to realise that the cosmos might not be something hierarchical and stable at all. We'd realise how much we had fallen into the trap of believing that all it took for healing to take place, was to stop or somehow extract any destructive agents.

10 Egyptian saying, source: *The Maxims of King Khety to His Son Merikare,* in: Lichtheim, 1973

Maybe this was one of the many lessons the Covid-19 crisis was meant to remind us of: That a deep understanding of true balance is different from attempting to contain or kill any aggressor to the status quo. This crisis offered us a vantage point on the scales of Ma'at: One from which we come to see that balance is not automatism of an organic nature, but a state that can only be maintained through the conscious collaboration of all living components of its ecosystem.

Both as humans as well as a hive of species in this world we will always fail in such noble aspiration, which is why our work is never done. *Speaking Ma'at, doing Ma'at* thus is the ultimate act of courage and commitment: To stride out into the world each day, to see the vast horizon of success for all things mundane as well as divine, and yet to accept our own inadequacy on the journey.

This is what the reformation of the world would have looked like through the eyes of the Egyptians: Not like a single heroic act, but as an ocean of tiny, daily heroic acts coming together from all species populating this sphere with us.

This also is what the Reformation could look like in our eyes, if only we chose to adopt such a worldview.

This would be a worldview in which acting begins with listening, with patience and observing, with joining together each deed as a promise that requires a counter-promise, with understanding living as weaving together yesterday and today, the last moment and then the next. Wouldn't that be quite a noble way of living?

This is, in fact, the way of the Adept, to walk with open hands, without a single step hidden away from the world, but out and into it, unrestricted, into its broad horizon. *Speaking Ma'at. Doing Ma'at.*

Becoming Gold

Reform: to convert into another and better form,
from Latin *reformare, to form again, change, transform, alter*

Reformation: improvement, alteration for the better,
from Latin *reformationem* (nominative *reformatio*)

Homo homini lupus est. Man is a wolf to man.[1]

The Inner Firmament.

Most reformations fail. Not because they are unable to overthrow the orthodox power structures they aim to break away from, but precisely because of what follows on once that goal is achieved. No sooner are individuals liberated from the oppression of secular or spiritual institutions, than they find themselves confronted with an unaccustomed level of liberation difficult to live up to. No matter how oppressive it may have been, once the scaffolding of common rules and regulations has suddenly fallen away, there is little to reduce the vast horizon of personal freedom to a manageable set of choices that individuals can cope with and agree upon. Most reformations fail, as Steven Ozment concluded so succinctly, "because they aim to ennoble people beyond their capacities."[2]

This is a hard truth to realise, and an even harder one to accept, especially as many reformations initially do not hold a highly aspirational program. Often they start humbly, with the simple ideal to liberate people from the suppressive yoke of ubiquitous authority. Unfortunately, they are prone to fall prey to the naive assumption

---

1 Latin proverb
2 Ozment, p. 438

that once this initial goal is achieved everyone will instantly be ready to live "simple sober lives, prey not to presumption, superstition, or indulgence, but merely as human beings."[3]

However, such a seemingly simple wish, to liberate individuals' capacity to live a simple and sober life, not as a heroine or a holy man but as an honest human being, proves most difficult to fulfill. For most of human history, it has been met with disappointment, though it formed the false implicit assumption of hundreds, if not thousands of well-meaning revolutions. Reformations fail not because collective change wasn't possible, but because we, the individuals, are neither prepared nor equipped to deal with their theoretically *positive* consequences. Too much good brings out the devil in us. Or to speak with Pelagius, the greatest gift Divinity made to man is the very substance with which he poisons himself: Free will.

> *[…] Ihr wisst, dass im Leib ein Geist ist; nun gedenkt wozu er nutze sei? Allein dass er den Leib erhalte, wie die Luft die Geschöpfe vor dem Ersticken bewahrt; also verstehe auch den Geist. Dieser Geist ist im Menschen den anderen Geistern wesentlich und sichtbar, greifbar und empfindlich. Und diese Geister sind miteinander verwandt wie ein Körper dem anderen. Ich habe einen Geist, der andere hat auch einen. Die Geister kennen einander wie wir; sie üben ihre Sprache miteinander wie wir, aber unberührt von unserer Rede, sondern ihrem eigenen Willen nach. […] So merke dass diese Geister nicht von der Vernunft geboren werden, sondern allein vom Wille, daher scheide voneinander den Willen und die Vernunft. […] Also merke, dass jene, die den vollkommenen Willen haben und zeigen, die gebären in ihrem Innern einen wesentlichen selbst erschaffenen Geist. Dieser wird nicht zugegeben oder verordnet dem Menschen aus dem Himmel, jener macht ihn selbst, wie ein Feuer aus dem Kießling gemacht wird, also wird durch den Willen dieser Geist auch gemacht. Und je nachdem der Wille ist, so ist auch der Geist beschaffen.[4]*

---

3 Ozment, p. 438

4 Paracelsus, in: Sudhoff, volume I, p.217/218

> *[...] You know that there is a spirit in the body; now think what it is good for? Only that it preserves the body, as the air preserves the creatures from suffocation; so also understand the spirit. This spirit in man is essential and visible, tangible and sensitive to the other spirits. And these spirits are related to each other as one body is to another. I have a spirit, the other also has one. The spirits know each other like we do; they practice their language with each other like we do, but untouched by our speech, but according to their own will. [...] Notice, then, that these spirits are not born of reason, but of the will alone; therefore, separate from each other the will and the reason. [...] So notice that those who have and show the perfect will, they give birth to an essential self-created spirit within themselves. This is not given to or bestowed upon man from heaven, he makes it himself, as a fire is made from a flint, so through the will this spirit is also made. And depending on the nature of the will, so is the spirit.* [5]

Paracelsus also spoke of two firmaments circling around the human flame residing in every human's heart: An outer firmament installed in the night sky, and an inner firmament infused in each individual's nature. While there are dependencies between these two firmaments, they are not at all locked into each other. Significant degrees of variation and freedom exist between outer and inner firmament. Thus our work to investigate, understand and ultimately live in harmony with *both skies* is not one and the same; rather, according to Paracelsus, as magicians we ought to walk in parallel paths, one on the inside, one on the outside, mutually enriching each other, and yet essentially different in their tools and trades.

Now, it would be unwise to believe one could find the essence of the outer sky, as well as the magical path leading towards it, in its most obvious symbolical representation, the astrological zodiac. It is true that Paracelsus's writings are steeped in what he called astronomia and the all-permeating influence of the stars and the celestial realm

---

[5] Paracelsus, in: Sudhoff, volume I, p.217/218

upon nature and man. Even the title of his *Meisterstück*, the *Astronomia Magna* (1537/1538) reminds everyone of the primary importance of the stars in his cosmology. And yet, as so often with the writings of this genius, a deeper meaning is revealed upon more careful reading.

Paracelsus divides the science and art of the regulating influence of the stars – the terms *astrologia* and *astronomia* were still used interchangeably in the 16th century - into four separate orders[6]:

- The first focuses on the influence of the stars on the entire microcosm, i.e. the body of earth (*Astronomiae Naturalis*);
- the second relates to those who work through *faith*, in Paracelsus' sense of the practice of visionary magic and the specific application of the celestial forces in vision (*Astronomiae Olympi Novi*);
- the third derives from Jesus Christ and is to be mastered by the mystics following his path (*Astronomiae Supera*);
- and finally the fourth category relates to the infernal spirits (i.e. chthonic beings of the underworld) who, as Paracelsus states, are themselves masters of astronomy (naturales astronomi) and thus need to be approached as equals by the magician (*Astronomiae Inferorum*).

Many good books have been written on classical astrology, or *Astronomiae Naturalis*. In *Holy Heretics* (Scarlet Imprint, 2021) I provide a careful exegesis of the underlying principles and practices of the order of *Astronomiae Supera* as well as of *Astronomiae Olympi Novi*. Furthermore, in *Clavis Goêtica* (Hadean Press, 2021) I have given an introduction to the pathways leading through the order of *Astronomiae Inferorum*. The interested student, therefore, is surrounded by open doors opening onto all four of these magical realms.

Returning to our original differentiation of the outer and the inner firmament in Paracelsus's work, we know that the outer *astronomiae* is not to be confused with classical astrology alone (*Astronomiae*

---

6 Peuckert, 1965, volume III, pp. 107

Naturalis). Rather, as far as authentic Paracelsian magic is concerned, *astronomiae* should be understood as the real capacity to achieve spirit contact. Whether we choose to tune into the natural world, the chthonic depths, the celestial heights or the silent heart-flame of Divinity, *astronomiae* describes the cosmic agency needed to facilitate inter-dimensional dialogue and exchange; exchange, not only of ideas, knowledge, power or services, but far beyond that, of ways of being, that is, an exchange of ontologies. The rhythm that defines who or what we are can be tuned and altered by the wise use of astronomiae. In this manner, the term ceases to define a unique discipline, and rather points to an understanding of astronomiae as both a physical as well as subtle *field*.

In light of this context of the outer firmament, what then, we might ask, is the practice and wisdom of the inner firmament? I have already proposed an answer in *Holy Heretics*, specifically in the long fifth chapter, 'The Call'. Here I'd like to shine a light from a different angle on this tricky question. One that might teach us more about mastering the spirit born from will: *How can we take ownership for the ways we hold ourselves towards the world, so that we can live a life as human beings in balance with Ma'at.*

None of us have control over failure or success of the next social revolution; however, nobody but we hold the reins over the reformation of our own selves. In true Pelagian spirit, and despite or maybe because of his many personal ethical shortcomings, Paracelsus remained a lifelong proponent of the individual's responsibility for their own life and of mastering the firmament within the self as an essential point of embarkation on the path of wisdom.

In late 1536, while setting out to write his magnum opus, the *Astronomia Magna*, Paracelsus seemed tired not only of his lifelong travels, but also of the general stupidity of mankind. Unable to earn much of a living, let alone to publish any of his more serious works, he turned to writing annual horoscopes, which were released as small pamphlets.[7] In the introduction to the annual horoscope of 1537, the mature adept offers a pungent taste of how far away at the time even the wise seemed from mastering the art of *astronomia* in their everyday lives.

> *Es ist ein Sprichwort bei den Gelehrten, wo ein weiser Mann herrscht, der überwindet das Gestirn. Demnach wären der Weisen wenige in dieser Zeit. Denn wenn man alle Dinge ausmisst, abwägt und betrachtet, so tut der Mensch eben das was der Himmel will und noch mehr. Wo der Himmel ein Quäntlein einflöst, da macht der Mensch zehn Pfund daraus und ist also noch ärger als der Himmel einem anzeigt oder eindrückt. Es ist etliche Jahre her dass die Planeten so vergiftet erschienen sind, wie es auf Erden hergegangen ist; der Mensch ist aber dermassen geneigt, dass wenn leicht ein Fünklein in ihn fällt, er viel weiter greift als das Fünklein anzeigt und führt. Denn obgleich wohl Mars etwas ein wenig anzündet, so übertreibt der Mensch es ohne Mass und Ziel und kann nicht zu viel daran tun. Er versteht es, sich selbst noch unflätiger zu machen, den Krieg, Zank, Hader in alle Länder, Städte und Dörfer zu bringen, selbst in seine eigenen Häuser. Also so auch Luna eine kleine Angel in einen einhängt für eine einzige Stunde, so lügt derselbe zehn Jahre lang danach, obgleich sie ihn gar nicht mehr berührt. Also mit der Venus: So sie kaum eines Gerstenkorn gross bei einem ist, so tut derselbige gleich als habe er von der Venus gefressen, und ebenso ist es mit den anderen Planeten. Mit dem Jupiter sind viele, die sich unter ihm wähnen, mit denen er gar nicht zu schaffen hat. Ebenso wähnen sich viele unter dem Merkur, die er über lange Jahre nicht gekannt hat. Also übertreibt es der Mensch und es ist weder Mass noch Ziel in ihm, weder Heben noch Legen. Obgleich der weise Mann den Himmel bezwingen soll in seinem [inneren] Firmament und seinen Neigung, tut er doch böses, macht Krieg und Blutvergiessen, wo keines sein soll, lügt, wo er nicht [von den Sternen] genötigt wird, sondern nur leicht angetastet wie ein Kamel von einer Fliege. So finden sich nun der Weisheit keine weisen Männer; denn solche sollten die [astrologischen] Neigungen,*

---

7 Will-Erich Peuckert, in: Sudhoff, volume XI, xxiv

Eindrücke, und Einflüsse von sich abschütteln wie ein Esel die Viehfliegen und wie ein Ross die Hornissen.[8]

•

It is a proverb among scholars that where a wise man rules, he overcomes the stars. Accordingly, the wise would be few in this time. For when all things are measured, weighed and considered, man does just what heaven wills and more. Where heaven makes a pittance, man makes ten pounds out of it, and so is even worse than heaven indicates or imprints. It has been some years since the planets appeared as poisoned as things actually appeared on earth; but man is so inclined that when a tiny spark easily falls into him, he reaches much further than the small spark indicates and leads. For although Mars may ignite something a little, man overdoes it without measure or aim and cannot do too much with it. He knows how to make himself even more obscene, to bring war, quarrels, strife into all countries, cities and villages, even into his own houses. So also Luna hangs a small fishing rod into one for a single hour, so the same one lies for ten years afterwards, although she does not touch him at all any more. So with Venus: If she is hardly the size of a barleycorn with one, then he acts as if he had gorged from Venus, and it is the same with the other planets. With Jupiter there are many who think they are under him, with whom he has nothing at all to do. Likewise many imagine themselves under the Mercury, which he did not know for many years. So man overdoes it and there is neither measure nor aim in him, neither lifting nor laying. Although the wise man should conquer the heavens in his [inner] *firmament and inclination, yet he does evil, makes war and bloodshed where there should be none, lies where he is not compelled* [by the stars], *but is only lightly touched like a camel by a fly. So now wise men are not found by wisdom; for such should shake off the* [astrological] *inclinations, impressions, and influences from themselves like a donkey the cattle flies and like a horse the hornets.*[9]

---

8 Paracelsus, in: Sudhoff, volume XI, p.227/228

9 Paracelsus, in: Sudhoff, volume XI, p.227/228

To *lift* or *lay* the influence of the stars, to absorb or amplify what the outer heaven is offers to man, rather than turning to the riotous and blind plaything of one's own inclination, according to Paracelsus, is the foundation of mastering the inner firmament, and so to stride out on the path of wisdom. Furthermore, the adept is giving us another hint – or is it a flat smack in the face? – at what is most required to accomplish such balanced co-existence with the stars: *To have a measure of and to hold an aim for oneself.*

Sometimes the key to unlocking magical texts is to anchor oneself deeply into a single sentence or expression. Paracelsus twice emphasis that man does "what heaven wills and more" because there is "neither measure nor aim in him".

By way of illustrating what Paracelsus might have meant by the word aim, I offer the following exercise. I invite you to do this exercise right here and now; it has the potential to change, whether subtly or indeed profoundly, the life still ahead of you, just as it once changed mine many years ago.

Seeing your Old Self

- Find a quiet place to sit or lie down. Make sure you will not be disturbed in the next hour. Also, ensure you have a glass of water and something to take notes with. Keep a small light on; operating in complete darkness will not work for this exercise.

- Relax yourself in whatever manner you choose. Observe how your breath slowly calms down. Let go of whatever experiences you just came from. Whatever happened before you sat or lied down in this place was then, and now is now.

- What you will do next marks a potentially important moment in your life. Show respect for the experience you are about to create for yourself. Most likely, you will only do this exercise once in your life. Smile for a moment and open your heart, for it will be whatever it will need to be. All you can do is to be present in a way that honours this moment.

- Now close your eyes. Imagine you are lifting yourself out of your own body. You float up to the ceiling, through the ceiling, up into the rafters, through the roof and into the sky. For a moment, you only hover weightlessly. Below you, you can see the house in which your body resides. Try to broaden your vista from this height, see the world stretch in all directions around you.

- Then, as if you are riding on a gush of wind, you find yourself carried forward. While flying ahead you realise this wind is not carrying you through space, but rather through time. You are rushing forward in time, years flying by unseen. You are as an arrow shot from its bow into the air – nothing can stop your flight.

- Finally you slow down and arrive at the presence of the future. Now you begin to descend from high above towards the earth. You realise the outlines of the land below you. It could be open land, a village, or a crowded city to which you descend. Your are confidant that you vision will guide you. You allow your mind to see the entire place clearly as you descend into it.

- Arriving at level ground, you look around.

- There, quite far from where you have descended, you see the outline of a person standing. While you cannot see them clearly, you realise this is your self grown old. But this isn't just one of many possible versions of yourself in your final days, rather it's the best possible one, a vision of you as you would most like to become, a version of you able to could look back in satisfaction at a life well spent: Standing there in the future is your old yet noble self.

- Slowly you are floating towards that person. Do not rush this process, allow it to take all the time it needs. And while you float towards your older self, pay attention to what you sense while you approach. How does that person look? What is that they exude? How are they present? How do they stand in this world, and in their final days?

- As you draw close to your old self, honour this moment, for you will not see each other again for a long time. Take this presence in, like a treasure you were granted. When you are ready, say goodbye, even though they might not hear you.

- A gentle but firm force lifts lifts you up. The same wind that had pushed you into the future, now pulls you back. It lifts you up into the sky, the scenery below you disappears, and you are rushed back through time, further and further, until you arrive in the present moment again.

- You find yourself in the sky above your house once more. You see the same scenery as before, nothing has changed. Whether you were gone for a second or for years, nobody knows. Gently you descend towards the house, and pass through its roof, rooms and ceilings, until you arrive in your own body again.

- Lie still and take a few deep breaths. Then stretch yourself. Allow your physical senses to wake up again and your inner and outer bodies to merge.

- Take up the pen and paper and write down everything you have learned about your noble old-age self. How did you appear? Which qualities did you perceive first, which ones later on? How did that person make you feel? And if you looked through their eyes at the world, what would you see that you are not seeing now?

There is no more important decision in life than how we want to die. That single aim should define how we live our lives.

With the risk of deviating, let's explore this idea for a moment more through an alchemical metaphor borrowed from real life: To this day we don't really know where gold comes from; but we do know how long and arduous its journey is before it arrives at the surface of earth. Following a 2017 study from the University of Granada, gold emerges over millennia, "from the deepest regions of our planet. Thus, the Earth's set of internal movements would have favored the ascent and concentration of the precious metal."[10]

The inside of the earth is divided into three broad sections, the inner nucleus, the mantle and the outer crust. All human activity happens on the outermost layer of the crust. The mantle begins roughly 70 kilometres underneath the continents and 17 kilometres below the bottom of deep ocean trenches. Reaching the mantle is impossible for humans, and yet the mantle itself finds ways to make contact with us. Either through millions of years of tectonic shifts or through volcanic eruptions, the molten minerals caught and concentrated in the mantle can reach the surface of the crust. The inside of earth's mantle is still much of a mystery; its general conditions can perhaps best be described as literally infernal: Temperature ranges from 200° to 4000° Celsius and pressure varies from a few kbar to 1390 kbar (139 GPa), which equals about 1.3 million times the atmospheric pressure. The scientists from the University of Granada propose that some 170 to 140 million years ago the conditions in certain areas of the mantle allowed for the accumulation of larger gold deposits. Since then, if we look at this as an alchemical allegory, the gold has been on its journey from the earth's infernal womb to the daylight on its surface, or in other words, from its inception to its birth.

How far are we prepared to go to live our lives with clear, enduring purpose? This means not stacking up days upon days without measure or aim, as Paracelsus warns us against, but rather intentionally adding page upon page, until the book that we have become tells a narrative that proves life worthwhile.

---

10 Science Daily; *Scientists reveals the mystery about the origin of gold*, 21st of November 2017, www.sciencedaily.com/releases/2017/11/171121095128.htm

Starting with the end in mind is a powerful technique to find such deep purpose: Looking at our selves in the future, when we are much closer to stepping into our grave, represents a moment of quintessential truth. Who have we become? What kind of inclinations have we imprinted upon ourselves? What is it, in the end, that will most define our presence? None of the outer accomplishments of our lives will matter at that point; they quickly fall to the wayside of change. What remains, what will be with us inside our grave, is the final version of ourselves who, through this work we have become.

Life is quarry from which we mine ourselves. The problem is this process happens so slowly, so gradually, that we are constantly distracted by the assault of the outer firmament. Rarely do we become conscious witnesses of the creation of our own inner firmament. Yet, whether the shape we have become in that final moment, fills us with joy, whether it lights our heart's flame and pulls us forward into another good life, that is down to the thousands of younger versions of ourselves we have blindly burned through, one day at a time.

Let us, for a moment, be as gold, deep inside the earth's infernal mantle. Let's breath deeply, and do not rush. Let's assemble ourselves, surrounded by tides of mysteries and unknown compounds, exuding constant pressure upon us. Let's collect ourselves, become deposits of gold, surrounded by darkness. Let's become gentle and patient enough for a path that will be long, as long as our entire life, and longer still. Only then can we set one foot in front of the other, one day at a time, with clear measure and aim in mind.

Seeing our old self empowers us to take control of our lives. Through this vision we can fashion every single day as a step on the journey that will ultimately lead us to becoming that man or woman. Choices of career, of family planning, of relocation or financial investments - they can then all be tied back to becoming this old version of ourselves. Rather then asking what it will take to achieve a certain professional position or pay-grade, the question becomes, how would things contribution to pulling that future self from the womb of earth? If I pursued this job, if I founded a family, if I relocated to that place marked X, which character traits would these experiences bring out in me, and are they in line with the face that I saw in my old self? If we consider each day a chisel and a hammer set upon the stone that we are, are our days chipping away stone at the right places to finally turn us into our old self? At the edge of our grave nothing else will matter but how we engaged in life, in order to leave it in a version of ourselves with whih we are in peace.

So, to start at the end, to turn yourself into black soil, a black god, and back into a mortal again, there is only one question worth wrestling with. And that is: which virtues are you willing to draw out of yourself?

> [...] *daß aber das Gold in dem Element des irdischen Feuers nicht verbrennt noch zerstört wird, ist das die Ursache davon, die Beständigkeit des Goldes. Es mag ein Feuer das andere nicht verbrennen oder verzehren, sondern so Feuer und Feuer zusammen kommen, wird es nur größer und stärker in seiner Wirkung. Das himmlische Feuer, das von der Sonne einfließt bei uns oder im Erdreich gewirkt wird, ist nicht ein Feuer, wie es im Himmel ist, [es] ist auch nicht wie unser Feuer auf Erden, sondern das himmlische Feuer ist bei uns ein kaltes erstarrtes und gefrorenes Feuer. Und dies ist der Leib des Goldes, darum mag man dem Gold mit unserem Feuer nichts abgewinnen, denn allein das man es damit zertrennet und fließend machet, gleich wie die Sonne den Schnee und das gefrorene Eis und Wasser aufweicht und fließend macht. Und darum ist dem Feuer nicht Gewalt gegeben Feuer zu verbrennen, weil Gold selbst Feuer ist. Im Himmel ist es gelöst, aber bei uns gebunden.* [11]

•

> [...] *but that the gold in the element of the earthly fire does not burn nor is destroyed, this is the cause of it, the permanence of the gold. One fire may not burn or consume the other, but when fire and fire come together, it only becomes greater nd stronger in its effect. The*

---

11 Paracelsus, in: Sudhoff, volume XIV, p. 413

heavenly fire, which flows in from the sun into our sphere or is worked in the earth, is not a fire as it is in heaven, [it] is also not like our fire on earth, but the heavenly fire in our sphere is a cold solidified and frozen fire. And this is the body of gold, therefore nothing can be gained from gold with our fire, but that it is cut and made fluid, just as the sun softens and makes fluid the snow and the frozen ice and water. And therefore fire is not given power to burn fire, because gold itself is fire. In heaven it is dissolved, but with us it is bound.[12]

---

12 Paracelsus, in: Sudhoff, volume XIV, p. 413

Postscript

Osiris is a black god.

Back in 2008 before I made contact with my Holy Daimon, I spent an entire year praying to a beetle. I had made a statue of *Khepri* and kept it in my temple in an old barn next to our house. Only I could enter that barn. Each time I did I brought offerings to the god dwelling in the statue. I prayed in front of the beetle almost every day for many months with a single thought on my mind: I gave the god of rebirth permission to apply its powers to myself; I asked it to take me to the grave and to bring me back in a version closer to my old, noble self. At that time I didn't know what that process would actually look like, and there simply was no need for me to know. In a sense, I was like the dreamer who surrenders to the dream; once one makes the decision to enter sleep everything else becomes simply a matter of following what comes.

After a full cycle of twelve months of adoration of *Khepri*, I completed the only Egyptian rite I ever practiced. After that I buried the statue of *Khepri* in an old wooden box, together with ritual offerings and a sigil confirming the pact we had made during the rite. Soon afterwards I took on a new job that shifted my entire life. New people, ideas, values and practices broke into my life as if set free by an earthquake. In my naivety I thanked *Khepri* and thought this was his answer to my prayers. Little did I know this was just the beginning.

Another twelve months later I worked upstairs in the old barn for many days. A new ritual cycle was calling, one that among German speaking adepts is called *Saturn Exerzitium*, and about which I have reported at length in my book *Holy Daimon* (Scarlet Imprint, 2018). Over four weeks of continuous practice this spiritual exercise builds up to a rite of symbolic death, a rite of passage. For this I had to craft my own full-sized coffin.

While every other tool of this ritual is long gone, buried deep in the Bavarian forests as part of my transition to the empty handed path, that coffin still rests in the attic of our house. I remember when we moved in - my wife explaining to the movers I was working in a theatre group and this was part of the props. And yes, that heavy, two-and-a-half metre long beast of solid black wood did need to go all the way up to the attic through that small trap door. After all there is humour even in the artefacts of our dying.

It was in that coffin that I first saw my Holy Daimon. It was also in that coffin that I first experienced alchemy as a physical process worked upon ourselves by angels. There is really nothing subtle to it, once one experiences it for real. Dreams, memories of distant lovers, of childhood enemies are subtle compared to it. I still remember the process as vividly as if it happened yesterday.

Again, I was naive enough to believe that upon leaving that coffin the process had been accomplished; I left that adorned, black box feeling like a phoenix rising from ashes. It was the same old me, but a me that now had access to the undying parts of myself. Little did I understand at that time, that any experience in ritual requires a subsequent experience in real life. To keep the scales of inner and outer worlds balanced, going through death in ritual required me to do the same - or almost so - in real life. Even as adepts we cannot create a reality for our souls and minds, that does not attract sympathy in the flesh into which we are bound. Once the door is opened, it is all of us, flesh, blood, bones, mind and soul, that must pass through it, and each in its own way.

A few years later I began preparing to face my biggest challenge yet, that of crossing the *Abyss*. The actual rite, the actual vision of passing over the Abyss, was almost effortless. These pathways have been walked by adepts for centuries, millennia. So once sufficiently trained it is not hard at all to see and follow them. Like signing a contract, putting your wet signature on the paper isn't a big deal. The deal is what follows.

After more than six years of active magical work on the theme of death and rebirth, it was surely time for me to allow it to become flesh. I was diagnosed with testicle cancer at a pretty late stage. Emergency surgery. Hospital, doctors' talk, scans hung on a wall, and a few very calm conversation about some pretty uncomfortable scenarios I had to face when leaving the hospital.

Yet, learning how to die before dying isn't done in a single hospital stay. As hard as it might seem in that moment. Confronting death is a first stage; learning how to live with its constant presence requires many subsequent stages to pass through. It took time for my mind to accept death as a travelling companion under my own skin; I moved slowly, through good days and bad, like gold trapped deep in the earth's mantle.

And so I am back to my cancer treatment scans every couple of months for several years now. Each time like any other patient I need to sit and wait in the radiologist's waiting room and drink a whole litre of milky fluid over the exact timespan of an hour. And each time I sit there, I put my heart back on the scales of *Ma'at*. I offer myself up to her and her soul-eating demon *Ammit*. I have asked for this. To learn how to die while still alive. This is my path and I walk it. Into death and out of it again, another step closer to my noble self; like a playground swing, back and forth, until the day it stops.

Lying on my back, arms above my head, the needle in my hand, feeling the contrast fluid pumping into my blood and circulating slowly through a large scanning machine, I know where I am. I am back in my coffin. These are my Osiris moments. And it is not upon me to decide whether or when I will be re-awakened.

All my teenage years I wondered what Eliphas Levi meant when he wrote to Baron Spedalari: *Osiris is a black god*. Now I know it. Every rite of rebirth requires many rites of dying. To cross the Abyss is a single act of magic. To accept its consequences in our lives invokes a looping spiral of events. Rewriting our inclinations, turning them into virtues, requires repeated carving, until they become a sensual pattern bound into our blood. We don't materialise the presence of our Holy Daimons through words and reflections; we bring them forth through our human senses. This is how s/he becomes one with us: Through every sensual experience we make. That's why the future self we have asked to become is pressing down the needle hard if new qualities are to be inked into us, so that, in the end they outlast our dying.

Opposite page: crafted coffin, pupose built for the four week long 'Saturn Exerzitium', in which I first encountered my Holy Daimon.

Chapter 2.

Authentically Angelic

Introduction

And mortal man is not worthy for him to see the spiritual angels: Because if the soul is polluted in the body, it cannot have tongues with the angel, yet if it was to have tongues, so it ought to be pure like the angels. (...) For this reason this rule is to be regarded as the highest secret and mystery [:] that one desires from their good angel that he may reveal to us and share his good thoughts. Because it is the office of the angels to be supportive of generating both the divine and human mind in man.[11]

The central theme in Johannes Trithemius's magical program coincides with the high goal of Ancient Western Magic since time immemorial: To instigate a change in the nature of humanity, whether this was considered a process of slow approximation, of sudden alchemical transformation or of reinstatement in the afterlife, that ultimately allowed for man's return into the sphere of the divine.[12]

In Ancient Egypt such processes were considered innately elitist and were reserved for the pharaohs alone. Similarily, originally in Greece it was a privilege of the mythical founding fathers of the nation, the ancient heroes, to be elevated to semi-divine status during their life times. Slowly over time in both cultures, however, the process became democratised.

Civic upward assimilation is a powerful force in any society; give it enough time and original elite privileges will erode and become commoditised. In the process they also become commercialised: Smart middle-men establish themselves as gateways and turn ancient

---

11 Pelagius Eremitae, aka Johannes Trithemius
12 Brann, 1999, p. 114-115

privileges into products for the masses, selling them off to the highest bider in promise of a more lasting gratification and recognition than monetary wealth can offer alone.

Of course, by the time such process reach the middle class they will have bled most of the mystical numen and integrity that perfused their original versions. What is sold, more than anything, is a memory-link, a romantic portrait of what once was a living reality. When it comes to apotheosis (i.e. deification in its Greek technical term), what the common man was offered was a distant echo at best of what the Greek heroes or Egyptian pharaohs enjoyed. Nevertheless, Prometheus always prevails.

And this precisely is the Promethean legacy of Trithemius' magical works: To restore an authentic Western version of making man perhaps not fully divine, but authentically angelic at least. To achieve this he had to do two things before everything else: To restore the path to an uncompromising, i.e. elitist practice again, and to trim back the many magical offshoots and additions that had crept up in the course of time and derailed the practitioner from the one and only goal of real value.

> *That during our days one does not see the angels anymore as one did long time ago, that stems from the fact that the good and pure angels cannot align themselves any longer to our impure manner and nature. So also our mind is too mean and weak that one cannot come close to the angels and become alike in union. In our weakness we have become separated from the good angels and are not deemed worthy of seeing them. Yet if we loved and feared God and acted according to the holy companionship so they would allow for to be seen by us.*[13]

If modern readers and practitioners step back and compare the essential premises hidden in Trithemius' magical works with the pathway to deification laid out by the Ancient Greeks, they will discover striking similarities. Maybe that is because Trithemius was such an avid reader of Greek myths and literature. Or maybe it is because

---

13 Pelagius Eremitae, aka Johannes Trithemius

spiritual reality doesn't follow tides and trends, and essentially remained the same over the two millennia that separate Trithemius and Homer.

In what follows we will examine four of these essential premises, shared between Trithemius's work and the implicit logic the Ancient Greek applied to what made (some!) women and men divine. These premises can be read as philosophical historic artefacts or as living stages on the path towards communion with our own 'angelic mind'. In this short overview we will refrain from examining technical details; and aim instead to shine a spotlight on the patterns that enable successful attempts of assimilation to the divine in the first place. The importance of being able to spot and identify such patterns, both in history as well as in one's own life, often outweighs many other technicalities. Re-tuning one's heart's compass can go a long way towards assimilating the ancient maps of spiritual ascent.

1. Nature Dictates

Fate is a pattern we are woven into by birth; fulfilling it, however, is a choice. None of the Greek heroes get to choose their origin story, instead they find themselves thrown into it by their very nature. While heroes always remain mortal, in many cases divinity is bound into their blood, as they are the direct offspring of a mortal and a deity or other spiritual being. Orpheus never got to choose the muse Calliope as his mother or to inherent her magical musical skills. Neither did Heracles choose Zeus as his father or to become an icon of masculinity, and Achilles didn't choose the nereid Thetis as his mother and to inherit her mesmerising beauty. This list could contain every human ever born, because whether our parents were deities or mortals, the same essential truth is woven into all of us.

Nature dictates the colour of our eyes, the length of the phalanges of our hands, as well as the particular skill within us that carries a divine spark. For some of us – the lucky ones – perfecting this skill naturally lights their heart up in passion; for others it becomes a life-long burden. Either way, none of us gets to choose the gift we are given by nature. And for all of us it is this particular skill that marks our unique pathway to reattach us to the divine. So in the end, the path to becoming god-like begins with an act of letting go. It begins with the cutting back of the abundance of possibilities and choices we feel surrounded by, especially in our youth. Instead, it begins with a voluntary subjection to a future version of our self which nature long ago placed as a seed within us. Such version of our self is not pre-determined in all its facets and traits, but in the particular art or craft it revolves around.

Orpheus dedicated a lifetime to perfecting the lyre; he didn't switch half-way through it into classical dance. Hercules overcame the seven trials through persistence and strength; he didn't give up after the fifth because he chose to become someone else. Nature dictates. The hero stays on the path. Understanding the nature of our own divine gift, and then choosing the life-long path of perfecting its expression, is the first step on the path of re-assimilating ourselves to our divine origins.

2. Quality Attracts

Once the Ancient Greek hero had sufficiently refined the expression of their divine gift, the gods became aware of them. And not a moment earlier. What captured the gods's attention, what hooked them into stepping closer to a particular mortal, was not the possible blood relation, and neither a romanticised ideal of ancestry or tribe. It was the spectacle of watching the hero perform their exceptional craft. The Greek gods were connoisseurs, constantly on the lookout for the kick provided by the excellent and exceptional, i.e. the marks that indicated a mortal had broken through the moribund bounds of earthly averageness.

In fact, broadly speaking, there were only four categories of qualities through which a hero could draw the attention of the gods upon themselves (Roloff, Gottähnlichkeit, p.31f). Of course, in rare cases a hero would be exceptionally gifted and perfect several of them. Yet, most of the ancient myths concentrate on a core quality for each hero, while mentioning others in passing:

- BEAUTY AND APPEARANCE: The hero may possess bodily beauty and grace of appearance as would dignify a god. This quality, especially for male warriors, also applied to mightiness and stature.
- PHYSICAL STRENGTH: A cardinal quality of the hero is physical strength. While still bound into a mortal body, the hero's prowess begins to converge with the realm of power reserved for the divine.
- PRUDENCE AND WISDOM: The hero may have an exceptionally strong ability to separate right from wrong, to cut through complexity and to always, even under the direst of circumstances, see a path that leads ahead. The hero is more than a leader; he or she has become almost as infallible in judgement as the gods.
- MAGIC AND SORCERY: Some heroes possess the gift of commanding the spirits, of enchanting nature and performing acts of sorcery otherwise reserved for non-human spirits and gods.

Obviously, such categories are highly artificial and reductive. They emerge from the field of classical studies and the literary evidence we hold of the Ancient Greek myths. Real life doesn't do bullet points and neither does it necessarily draw hard lines between categories of greatness. Instead, the point we take from studying the old myths is a much simpler one: The road to apotheosis begins with how we show up in the world.

Think of the fauna surrounding you. What attracts a bee is colour. What attracts a rat is scent. All animals follow invisible pathways of sympathy. Not because they choose to, but because they are bound to it. It is what nature dictates. The same principle is true for the spiritual and divine worlds: Spirits too are bound into laws of sympathy. Just like bees and rats and humans, they follow natural tides and patterns established by the resonance between their own nature and the surrounding environment. Some places make great hosts to them, others repel them – all happening not by choice, but defined by the resonance of qualities.

This is the second step on our path of becoming authentically angelic: To understand each act in the mortal world as an act of communication with the immortal one. This is what the mysterious messenger *Libanus* (aka Johannes Trithemius) alludes to when he mentions that most of all what he gained from his master Pelagius was 'a kind of natural dignity, which elevates'.

Imagine the physical world as the membrane of a drum. The stroke and rhythm with which we touch it, through every word we utter, through every deed we do it sends out a call of a most particular nature. It can only be heard and followed by the kind of spirits sympathize with the vibration of our call.

Do not be led astray by the Ancient Greek's obsession with beauty, strength, prudence or sorcery. These are mere possible byproducts of a much more essential choice: If you want to call for Neptune, what is the Neptunian stroke of the drum that is this world? If you choose to call for Venus, what is the Venusian touch upon the skin that is this world?

And if you call for the angelic world, where your Holy Daimon resides, which qualities should you perfect so s/he is called towards you, like the bee to the bloom?

> *It was with this Pelagius that I first realised how much in vain I had struggled in* [the art of] *magic without a teacher because in short it is impossible to understand her without a teacher. Because for the one who subjects themselves as Novice to the instructions of magic, it is imperative to acquire a kind of natural dignity, which elevates them, so that they may force the spirits of any kind to obedience. My teacher yet was radiant by a threefold virtue: that is of nature, of merit and*

of art. That is why he held all spirits which he desired at his will and in perfect control.[14]

3. Assimilation Enables

Now once the Greek gods spotted a human with extraordinary qualities they liked to get up close. Guess where all the semi-divine heroes come from? The stories of the Ancient heroes are stories of close encounters. Here we are dealing with the Greek world before the Platonic-turn that transformed all things physical into shadows and mere memory-images of their original ideas. In the world of the heroes before Xenophanes (d. 475 BC), the gods liked to appear in the flesh. And they liked to dwell in it – for as long as it had been sufficiently assimilated to their own.

Unfortunately, this still seems to be one of the most common misunderstandings in modern magic. From the days of Homer to Harry Potter, magic has always been a physical thing. Just because most of our mortal eyes cannot see into the spiritual realm, it does not mean that its forces do not constantly push into our tissue, membranes and cells. Ironically, nobody has the problem of understanding this 'corporal to non-corporal' relationship when it comes to electro-magnetic forces or nuclear radiation. We get that we cannot see it, but that it exists and powerfully affects the material world, including our bodies if we chose to contact it. Why is it so hard to see the same apply to the realm of the spirits?

If the world is the drum you play through your deeds and words and presence, then your body is the drum the spirits play through theirs. Learn to tune it, to listen to it, and you will know how to mend the instrument that plays between the human and the divine.

The Ancient Greek culture imagined all human capabilities to be derived from the gods. Interestingly, we find this same idea embedded in the Henochian myth of the fallen angels. Here the *Nephilim* descended to the mortal realm, and taught humans all crafts and

---

14 Libanus, aka Johannes Trithemius

arts. While these angelic gifts remained with the humans after the Nephilim were gone, the Greek version is different. According to it, not only do all human skills ultimately derive from the gods, but each time they are exercised the actual grace of the particular god is required for the skill's flawless expression.

While in the former myth the angelic-human relationship is an origin story of the ancient past, in the Greek culture it was a constant experience – just as much as a requirement to uphold it. In light of this, according to the Ancient Greek re-assimilating oneself to the divine was less about mental ascent than physical proximity. In essence, assimilation to the divine referred to a change in (spiritual) location, not in nature.[15]

If we consider the following not as an abstract (Platonic) concept, but a living physical reality we might better understand the nature of apotheosis: While the communion with a particular deity or spirit was the goal of apotheosis, assimilation was what formed the actual path. The separation of magical acts into 'evocations' versus 'invocations' is an 18th century folly. Standing in the presence of a powerful spirit will permeate our entire being all the way, periphery, surface, centre. In fact, it will permeate our presence and past, step over the threshold of time and intertwine with the path behind us and ahead.

Trithemius understood this all too well. We can still find his detailed knowledge of such encounters laid out in the Trithemian manuscripts we examined in *Black Abbot · White Magic*. Trithemius's works under the disguise of the magical hermit Pelagius are attempts to re-assimilate the nature of the neophyte to a divine nobility – one that is not born from the centre of the ritual, but from the meandering path of its periphery. That is also why identifying the precise name of one's good angel was thought to be of minor interest. What mattered immensely was the way the neophyte applied their heart and hand to the world. As soon as this operation succeeded it would automatically attract the right angelic being.

---

15 Roloff, 1970, p. 141

Ours is not the privilege of selecting and choosing with whom we will commune, Trithemius might have said; ours is the task of becoming a single, vibrant cell of noble intent. Once presence shines out into the mundane and spiritual worlds in such a manner – unbiased, undistorted – we do not need to worry which beings will answer our call. We will find ourselves being pulled forward, striding out unconstrained into the world, with our heart close to the throne. Authentically angelic.

4. Communion Elevates

In the Greek myths all forms of communion with a deity are temporary in nature. There is no such thing as a constant state of being united with a spirit or god – instead the spiritual bond requires constant rebinding, expressed e.g. through divine service, adoration or hymns.

Nature has a tendency to drift, to permeate and shape-shift. That is how evolution is kept alive. Nature is constantly drawn towards the unexplored, it breeds new forms and faces – by pulling away from and pulling apart what it had assembled just a minute ago. Nature thrives on carcasses; only they can offer the nourishing humidity for its new seeds to germinate and sprout. And once these have fully flourished, it will pull them back into the ground as well.

Cultivating a human-spirit relationship requires as much attention, skill and care as any human-to-human relationship does. And even in its best case, man will always remain a mortal. Believing one could forever turn oneself into a deity was folly even among the Ancient Greek. The flight of Icarus might be the most beautiful expression of such hubris. Already among the old heros apotheosis constituted a heresy, if it was understood as the human attempt to become a god for good (*Vergöttlichung*). Instead, what was an honoured mystical pathway was the pursuit of becoming god-like in a particular quality (*Gottähnlichkeit*) and thus garnering the favour and companionship of a particular deity.

Achieving communion with a particular spirit in most cases will form the pinnacle of decades of training and turning ourselves *alike*. Thus divine communion is a single moment in time quickly followed by others much more mundane ones. There is no standing still in the river of time. The same effort that is placed into mastering the art of creating divine proximity, should be placed into mastering the art of becoming fully human again.

Every time I depart from the place and presence of my Holy-Daimon is a moment of sadness. It is a moment that reminds me of the kindness of death, and the constant struggle that is our lives. Because there is no such kind of healing and peace as within my HolyDaimon. And yet just like Icarus it is not for me to stay too close to the sun for too long. – Once I had achieved communion with my HolyDaimon, learning how to come down from it was the hardest thing. After working for two decades to achieve this state of encountering Thou-I-Thou, why could it only last a few minutes at a time? Of course, I can sense my Holy Daimon around me even when not in communion. It is as simple as calling out to her/him. And yet, nothing compares to the experience of stepping inside her/his body in complete silence.

By definition all successful magical rites constitute peak experiences. And wherever there is a peak, there is a slope to both sides of it. If we want to learn to become authentically angelic, we better also become masters of being human. In fact, this is what I learned from my own conscious journey with my HolyDaimon over the last ten years: Once we had achieved communion s/he asked me to cease all practical magic. The door was open now, no more fiddling with the locks. All s/he wanted was for me to entirely apply myself to the mundane world around me… We have to understand: Rather than our holy daimon being an asset to us, really we are much more of an asset to them.

My return into the world of Malkuth, since we encountered each other in physical proximity, has become a journey of bringing her/his light through in everything I do. Today this is no longer a conscious effort. S/he is pushing through my skin, through the hollow of my mouth, the tip of my fingers wherever I walk or stand. I am no longer sure if I could stop this process? But I certainly have learned how to live with it in peace. And an essential part of this process is learning to step into communion with my HolyDaimon only sparingly.

Imagine you are Hercules and you have mastered the seven trials. Maybe your biggest challenge for the rest of your life remains not to apply all your strength to random things: To learn to drink from a glass without breaking, to learn to lift a sword without going to war or to learn to approach the unknown, and not to consider it a demon disguised.

Communion elevates. And with departure we descend. Both are stages in the process we have to master to become authentically angelic. We move on from communion to nourishing companionship (from Latin: *com = together* and *panis = bread*). From the moment where we are one, to the moment we stand side by side again – only then can we look each other in the eye, and break the bread of friendship.

> *You holy dear angel of God, for you are appointed over me to help and protect me and to shelter me, I laud, praise and honour you, I hold that God granted you to me as a companion and I delight in your amiableness and your service, for throughout my life you have protected me from much misfortune until this present day and hour. You dear, holy angel, I cannot repay you with any goods or deeds. You holy angel N.N., you blessed servant of God, for you behold God's face and take delight in standing in front of the face of God; I command myself to you [...].*[16]

---

16 Pelagius Eremitae, aka Johannes Trithemius

Chapter 3.

An Angelic Prayer by Karl von Eckartshausen

In the previous section we grounded ourselves in some essential thoughts on the art of becoming alike to the angelic mind. In the upcoming chapters (4 and 5) we will explore an unofficial magus degree ritual that emerged from the milieu of the *Order of the Gold and Rosy Cross* in the late 18th century.

Central to this text, published in the spirit of the original Rosicrucians, is the motto *The True and the Good* (*Das Wahre und Gute*). In fact, the author states that together with the number 75 and the word *Vaudahat* this motto was one of the keys that identified the mages in their order who worked from within the sphere of Tiphareth.

We will hear more of this in the following chapters. But first, let us consider the prayer presented here as a sacred bridge between the foregoing chapter and the next.

In 1791 one of the men I admire most published a book of rather unusual prayers. Towards the end of this book, when we ground ourselves again in the earth of Malkuth, we will hear more of him and depart with his words on *Prudence combined with Virtue*. I am speaking of Carl von Eckartshausen (1752-1803), a famous German mystic, philosopher, occultist and alchemist.

Most often today he is known as the author of the classic *The Cloud Upon the Sanctuary* (*Die Wolke über dem Heiligthum*, 1802), which influenced the early Golden Dawn and Aleister Crowley specifically.

Eckartshausen was also a highly successful lawyer, one of the youngest ever privy councillors at the Munich court, a Secret Archiver and member of the Bavarian Academy of Sciences. While he is listed as an early member of Carl Weishaupt's *Order of the Illuminati*, he quickly left it again and became a prominent critic of the order. His research mainly delved into mystical, kabbalistic and numerological studies.

Most of all, though, Eckartshausen was obsessed with understanding the human heart — and how to refine it. And this is where the above mentioned prayer book comes into play: Under the unassuming title *God is the Love most Pure*[17] and over almost three hundred pages, Eckartshausen masterfully wove his extensive occult knowledge and hermetic-rosicrucian meditations into what equally could be read as the reflections of a Christian natural philosopher. Much to everyone's surprise, the book became a stunning success and saw a huge volume of reprints well into the late 19th century.

And it is in this book, which was published roughly at the same time as our unofficial magus-grade ritual, that we come across a prayer titled *On the True and the Good (Über das Wahre und Gute)*.

•

In the following I am providing my personal translation of this short mystic prayer, followed by the German original. Like all prayers, it is meant to be spoken from the heart. Thus, we will refrain from providing a line by line analysis of the magical mysteries alluded to in it. To the careful reader, however, the short text will provide an invaluably concise summary of the practice of becoming alike to the angelic mind — spoken not from celestial heights, but from the headstone of Malkuth.

Finally, allow me to add the following few remarks on language: Wherever the word *knowledge* in English appears, the German original is *Erkenntnis* which equally translates as *gnosis*. Equally, the terms *mind* or *wit* are translations of the German *Verstand* which holds stronger connotations of the idea of *understanding* and even *prudence* than the English *mind* might do.

---

17 London: Hatchard, 1817; original: *Gott ist die reinste Liebe*, 1790

Here is to the true and the good in all of us. Surely, it is a time when we can all make use of some.

> *The influence of Eckartshausen and his work extended to all of Europe and was especially perceptible in Germany, England, France and Russia. His system, which is nevertheless in no way innovative, is testimony to a scope and a depth of vision that command admiration. This richness makes him, next to Franz von Baader, one of the most representative gems of Christian theosophy in the last two decades of the German 18th century.*[18]

---

18 Jaques Fabry, *Eckartshausen*, in: Hanegraaff, 2006, p. 328

On the True and the Good.

When I look around, my God! and behold the beautiful creation! when I consider your wise commands, All things call to me that truth and goodness are the pillars upon which heaven and earth rest.

It is therefore necessary, O God! that I know what is true and good; and it is this important subject that I will reflect upon today;

Truth and goodness are only you, and true and good is only what you are. Love in knowledge is the good, and love in practice is the true.

Truth and goodness must be united, for truth is an object of knowledge, and goodness is an object of will: And what would knowledge be without will?

The mind and wisdom of your angels, O Lord!, come into being through the union of the true with the good! without this union is only error and falsehood.

Truth, O God! therefore is you, and true is all that you are: So if I seek truth, I must seek you, become alike to you.

You gave me, my God, will and wit – the wit to know, the will to want what I have come to know. You, my God! are goodness: Everything that has being [German = Dasein] *is good, and everything true that comes close to the exercise of this goodness. When I recognize your goodness, and this knowledge passes into my will, then your goodness becomes visible through me, and my action is true.*

So let me realise, my God!, that I must combine the good with the true, and grant me your wisdom so that I may have understanding and will, and do not make me equal to the wise men of the world who have only science instead of understanding, and desire instead of will; you turn my will into the vessel of the good, and my mind into the container of the true. Amen.

Über das Wahre und Gute

Wenn ich umhersehe, mein Gott! und die schöne Schöpfung betrachte! wenn ich deine weisen Anordnungen erwäge, so ruft mir Alles zu, dass Wahrheit und Güte die Stützen sind, worauf Himmel und Erde ruhen.

Notwendig ist es also, o Gott!, dass ich wisse, was wahr und gut; und über diesen wichtigen Gegenstand will ich heute nachdenken;

Wahrheit und Güte bist nur du, und wahr und gut ist nur das, was du bist. Die Liebe in der Erkenntnis ist das Gute, und die Liebe in der Ausübung das Wahre.

Wahrheit und Güte müssen vereinigt sein; denn Wahrheit ist ein Gegenstand der Erkenntnis, und Güte ein Gegenstand des Willens: Und was wäre die Erkenntnis ohne den Willen?

Der Verstand und die Weisheit deiner Engel, oh Herr!, Entstehen durch die Verbindung des Wahren mit dem Guten! ohne diese Verbindung ist nur Irrtum und Falsches.

Wahrheit, o Gott! bist also du, und wahr ist Alles, was du bist: Wenn ich also Wahrheit suche, muss ich dich suchen, dir ähnlich werden.

Du gabst mir, mein Gott!, Willen und Verstand – den Verstand, um zu erkennen; den Willen, um das zu wollen, was ich erkannt habe. Du, mein Gott! bist Güte: Alles was ein Dasein hat, ist gut, und Alles wahr, was der Ausübung dieser Güte nahe kommt. Wenn ich deine Güte erkenne, und diese Erkenntnis in meinen Willen übergeht, dann wird deine Güte durch mich sichtbar, und meine Handlung ist wahr.

Lass mich also erkennen, mein Gott! dass ich das Gute mit dem Wahren verbinden muss, und gib mir deine Weisheit, damit ich Verstand und Willen habe, und lass mich den Weisen der Welt nicht gleich sein, die statt Verstand nur Wissenschaft, statt Willen nur Begierde haben; schaff du meinen Willen zum Behältnis des Guten, und meinen Verstand zum Behältnis des Wahren. Amen.

Chapter 4.

Bernhard Schleiß von Löwenfeld: Der höchste symbolische Grad der Magie. Ein hinterlassenes Manuskript eines Weisen an seinen Sohn.

[1] Anno 1774 den achtundzwanzigsten Juni übergab mir mein Vater ein verschlossenes Paket mit folgender Überschrift: Mein Sohn, öffne dieses Paket nicht eher, als in dem dreiunddreißigsten Jahre deines Alters an deinem Geburtstag – ich trage dir dieses bei dem Gehorsam auf, den du mir schuldig bist, würdest du es wider meinen Willen eher öffnen, so würden alle meine guten Absichten, die ich habe, da ich dir diese Papiere überreiche, vereitelt werden. Bist du aber gehorsam und erfüllst du meinen Befehl, so wird dich Gott segnen, und meine Absicht wird erreicht werden.

Nimm also dieses Paket, und verschliesse es in das eiserne Kästchen, daß ich dir schenkte, und lege die Kräuter dazu, die ich dir sagte – und vergrabe dieses Kästchen bei der großen Eiche im Breitwald, unweit der Kirche am Hügel, wo wir öfters saßen, vergrabe es drei Schuh tief, und jährlich sehe nach und lege frische Kräuter zum Papier, die dir bewußt sind, damit es nicht verwese.

Ich befehle dir dieses darum, damit diese Papiere nicht in die Hände eines Unwürdigen kommen möchten. Er würde zwar die Geheimnisse nicht verstehen, weil er das Chiffre nicht wüßte – doch ist es besser, wenn es gar nicht geschieht.

Nimm dieses Geschenk, lieber Sohn, von mir zu deinem zweiundzwanzigsten Geburtstage, und werde ich die Freude nicht mehr erleben, dir zu deinem dreiunddreißigsten Geburtstage Glück zu wünschen, so öffne dann das Paket, und nimm dann auch durch eine unsichtbare Hand meinen Segen jener Welt an.

•

Im Jahre 1785 den achtundzwanzigsten Junius hatte ich mein Kästchen, daß ich jährlich besuchte, öffnete es und fand in selbigen nebst einem nochmal verschlossenen Paket folgende Schrift.

•

Mein Sohn! Du bist nun in dem Alter des Mannes, und wenn du meinen Lehren, die ich dir in deiner Jugend gab, getreu warst, so wirst du würdig den großen Geheimnissen sein, die ich dich lehren werde. Von Jugend an hast du Freude mit seltsamen, und wunderlichen Dingen gehabt; allein du warst dort noch nicht in dem Alter, das reif genug war, dich mit höheren Geheimnissen der Natur bekannt zu machen, ich musste daher meine Lehre bis in dein reiferes Alter aufsparen, und daher händigte ich dir diese Papiere aus; wenn ich nicht mehr leben sollte, so werden sie dich unterweisen.

Bei diesem Paket, das du eröffnest, findest du noch ein verschlossenes – öffne solches nicht, ehe du zuvor gelesen hast, was hier geschrieben steht – ich beschwöre dich, denn es würde dich ins Verderben bringen.

Ehe du zu lesen weiter fährst, so werfe dich vor dem Unendlichen nieder und bete:

Gebet.

Du Gott meiner Väter, und barmherzigster Herr! Der du alle Dinge durch dein Wort erschaffen hast. [2] Und durch deine Weisheit verordnet hast, daß der Mensch über die Naturen, die von dir erschaffen sind, herrschen soll, daß er auch die Welt mit billig und Gerechtigkeit regieren, und mit aufrichtigem Gemüht urteilen soll.

Gib mir die Weisheit, die vor deinem Thron steht, und verwirf mich nicht von der Zahl deiner Diener.

Ich bin dein Diener, ein Sohn deiner Magd, und ein schwacher Mensch; ich kann ohne dir nichts, und alle Weisheit der Menschen ohne deine göttliche Weisheit ist Torheit in deinen Augen.

Sende mir also die Weisheit von deinen heiligen Himmeln, und von dem Thron deiner Hoheit herab, damit selbe immer bei mir sei, mit mir arbeite, damit ich weiß, was dir angenehm ist. Amen.

Wenn du nun dieses Gebet vollendet hast, so lese weiter:

Ich war, mein Sohn, aus der Gesellschaft der nach Weisheit strebenden. Unser Wahlspruch war: Wahrheit und Güte: unsere Zahl 75. Unser Wort: Vaudahat. Unsere Nomination Thiphereth: das verschlossene Paket wird das weitere erklären.

Das Symbol unserer Erinnerung sind vier Herzen, welche sich im Mittelpunkt konzentrieren, und die Form eines Kreuzes ausmachen, eine Kette vereinigt diese Herzen, und macht ein ganzes aus.

Dieses Symbol ist das Zeichen, das uns beständig an die hohe Pflichten des Menschen Berufes erinnern soll, welche ich dir weiter erklären werde.

Unsere Gesellschaft, lieber Sohn, hat mit keiner Gesellschaft, die je existierte, oder existiere eine Gemeinschaft – wir verbanden uns nicht durch Eidschwüre – wir haben weder Konstitutionen noch geschriebene Regeln, weder Konventen noch Logen, unsere Arbeit ist tätige Gottes- und Menschenliebe – Unser Orden ist der Orden Gottes – der Heiligen – der Magie – der Weisen.

Wir nehmen niemanden auf, jeder nimmt sich selbst auf nach dem Grad der Liebe, den er sich durch seine Handlungen gibt, nach diesem versetzt er sich in den höheren oder unteren Grad der Göttlichen Annäherung.

Wir haben keine Oberen, wir alle sind gleich untereinander – unser Vorstand ist Gott.

Wir halten keinen Sekretär noch Siegelbewahrer; der Engel, der die guten Handlungen der Menschen ins Buch der Ewigkeit einträgt, ist unser Sekretär, und unser Siegel, den wir führen, ist der Stempel der reinsten Absicht, der den Siegel der Liebe auf unsere Handlungen druckt.

Keiner hat den anderen zu gebieten; jeder gebietet sich selbst nach dem Grad seiner Erkenntnis.

Wir schliessen niemand aus, jeder schliesst sich selbst aus durch die Stufe der Entfernung, auf die er wieder hinunter steigt, wenn er Wahrheit und Güte verlässt.

Wir machen keinen Staat im Staat, sondern sind gute Menschen unter den Menschen.

[3] Bei uns sind keine Zeremonien; unsere Einweihung ist tätige Gottes- und Menschen-Liebe.

Wir lehren uns, ohne daß wir uns sehen, durch tätige Liebe an einander kennen, und nach der Reinheit der Liebe kennt jeder den Grad der Weisheit, den der andere hat.

Ehrenzeichen, Vorrang und besondere Vorzüge sind bei uns nicht, sie sind Kennzeichen der noch ungebildeten Arbeiten im Tempel Gottes; der Baumeister allein bestimmt unseren Wert, wir können uns keine Vorzüge zueignen, noch den Grad der Verdienste unserer Brüder bestimmen.

Die echten Maurer-Logen (aber sie sind wenige) sind Pflanzschulen, aus diesen tritt der Mensch, wenn er zur Erkenntnis kommt zu höherer Weisheit hinüber, er kommt aus dem Materiellen ins Geistige, oder aus dem sichtbaren ins unsichtbare.

Allein der junge Mensch, der auch kein Maurer, kann diesen Grad der Höhe erreichen, denn, wenn sein Wille gut ist, führt ihn Gott zur Weisheit.

Da sich der Materielle Mensch selten in die so große Wahrheiten hinein denken konnte, so glaubten unsere Vorfahren, man könnte den sinnlichen Menschen nach und nach zum nicht sinnlichen bilden, und daher verhüllten sie die Wahrheit großer Geheimnisse in Figuren, um stufenweise den Menschen zu Kenntnis zu führen, und so entstand die Maurerei.

Aber der polierte Stein, der die Wahrheit sagen will, bekam bald eine Klüfte, denn die Menschen arteten aus, und machten unechte Absichten zu ihren Zwecken und die Wahrheit verlor sich in Zeremonien.

So sind leider mein Sohn! noch die meisten Maurer-Logen heut zu Tage, sie versprechen den Menschen zum Licht zu führen, und tappen im Finstern herum.

Hüte dich also mein Sohn! und lasse nicht durch das äußerliche dein Auge blenden, sondern folge meinem Rat, und die Weisheit wird dich in ihren Schoß aufnehmen.

Der höchste Grad der Weisheit kennt kein Zeremonie – die Engel, die am nächsten an der Gottheit sind, sind nackt, das Kleid ist das Zeichen der Kenntnis unserer Blöße.

Ich führe dich auf die höchste Stufe des Tempels – ich will dir die Wahrheit in ihrem Licht zeigen, und ich reiße den sinnbildlichen Vorhang von ihrem Wohnsitz, der sie bisher in deinen blöderen Augen verhüllte, weil du vielleicht ihr Licht nicht hattest ertragen können.

Lerne mein Sohn die höchsten Stufen des Menschen Glückes keimen – dieses Glück ist das Wahre in der Erkenntnis und das Gute in der Ausübung – und genieße zugleich die Vorteile, die dir das Wahre und Gute gewahret.

Empfang das letzte Symbol des höchsten Grades der Magie, der ewig zu Erinnerung deiner höchsten Pflichten sein soll, und das ich dir hernach erklären werde.

(4) Du gehst nun in die Gesellschaft der Weisen über; in diesem Augenblick, in dem dein Wille fest, deine Liebe rein ist, bist du mit Ihnen verbunden, und ein Engel, den die Weisheit zu deiner Führung schickt, wird dich nun leiten, mache dich nie seiner Leitung unwür-

dig. Wir haben nun keine Zeremonien, mehr noch einen Tempel, – unser Tempel ist die Welt, unsere Zeremonien tätige Ausübung der Werke der Liebe.

Unsere Arbeit ist das Wahre und das Gute, und Wahrheit und Güte ist Weisheit; unser höchster Meister ist Gott, unser Mitarbeiter Engel und weise Menschen.

Unser Band ist das Band der Liebe, das den Menschen mit dem Menschen, und den Menschen mit Engeln und Gott vereint.

Mein Sohn! Ähnliches kettet sich an ähnliches – gleiches an gleiches – du bist nun nach dem Grad deiner Liebe mit deinem ähnlichen, mit deinem gleichen verbunden.

Du wirst, ohne zu wissen wie, mit Menschen von hoher Art bekannt werden, – denn weder Weltenheil noch Tod trennt den Weisen von dem Weisen – denn für ihn ist weder Raum noch Zeit.

Je mehr dich dein Geistliches aufschließt, je mehr wirst du übernatürliche Kenntnisse bekommen, du wirst von erhabenen Wesen geleitet werden.

In der Gesellschaft – in die du nun eintrittst, kannst du weder betrügen, noch betrogen werden – wo Wahrheit ist, hat das Falsche keine Probe – und Verstellung halt die Prüfung nicht aus.

Die Gesellschaft der Weisen ist die Rechnung, mit der das Unkraut von dem Korn getrennt wird.

Sie ist ein Haus, im welchem der Böse nicht wohnen kann. Du schließest dich selbst wieder aus, wenn du verächtlich wirst – wenn du dich vom Licht entferntest, so ist es wieder deine Schuld, wenn Blindheit die Augen deiner Seele dunkelt.

Gehe mit Muth und Zutrauen, ein unsichtbares Wesen wird dich leiten – die größten Geheimnisse der Natur, Wunder, Heilung wird dein Anteil sein. – Die Weisheit teilt diese Geschenke aus, und man empfängt sie ohne Neid, ohne Missgunst.

Ich erkläre dir nun, mein Sohn, das letzte und höchste Symbol.

Dieses Symbol besteht in 4 Herzen, die an einander gekettet sind. In der Mitte ist eine Rundung mit der Aufschrift: *Das Wahre*, Auf der andern Seite mit der Aufschrift: *Das Gute*. Die 4 Herzen sind das Quadrat der Liebe, wodurch alles bestehet.

Liebe Gott – deinen Fürsten und dein Vaterland – die Menschen deine deine Brüder, deine Feinde.

Liebe Gott ohne Eigenliebe – deinen Fürsten und dein Vaterland ohne Eigennutz – die Menschen deine Brüder, ohne Absicht auf Lohn, deine Feinde ohne Hoffnung, daß sie je deine Freund werden. Diese Zusätze charakterisieren den höchsten Grad der Liebe, und machen uns der Gottheit ähnlicher.

(5) *Der vordere Teil.*

Der hintere Teil.

Das reine Gold, aus welchem dieses Sinnbild gemacht ist, bedeutet die Reinheit unserer Seele, dessen sich der Mensch befleißigen soll.

Die Politur ist das Zeichen, daß man sich von allen Makeln reinigen soll, die verhindern könnten, das Licht der ewigen Sonne zu empfangen.

Die 4 Herzen an der Kette sind das Sinnbild der Liebe, der Mittelpunkt bedeutet die Gottheit, das 1. alles Guten – woraus alles kommt, wohin alles zielet.

Die Zahl 4 bedeutet die Dauer der Beständigkeit der Dinge – So ist die Zahl IV die Magie des Daseins – die Existenz – die Handlung – die Waage der Natur, nach welcher alles sich wiegt. Nimm also dieses Zeichen, mein Sohn, aus der Hand deines Vaters, und binde es mit einem feuerfarbenen Bande an deine Seite, und trage es zur beständigen Erinnerung deiner Pflichten.

Die Farbe des Bandes erinnere dich, daß dein Eifer nie erkalten soll, wie das Feuer deiner Liebe.

Reinige dein Herz, versammle deine Seele, wähle die Einsamkeit, und bete zu Gott – und mache dich würdig, den höchsten Grad der heiligen Magie zu empfangen.

Lasse das obige Symbol in einen Siegel stechen mit der Aufschrift: totum unitur amore – und bist du mit einem Guten im Briefwechsel, so wird er dich kennen, vergesse aber nicht, den Siegel wahrer Liebe in jeder deiner Handlungen zu drücken – denn was wäre das Sinnbild ohne Wahrheit.

Öffne nun das zweite Paket, und lerne aus selbem den Weg zu den grossen Geheimnissen nach der Chiffre, die ich dir nicht lernte, kannst du selber lesen, hast sie gelesen, so verbrenne sämtliche meine Papiere, und behalte die heiligen Geheimnisse nur in deinem Herzen.

(6) Diese meine Einleitung aber kannst du dir abschreiben, auch wenn du es nach deinem Zeitalter tauglich findest, den Liebhabern der Wahrheit mitteilen, um ihnen gesunde Begriffe wahrer Weisheit mitzuteilen. Die Geheimnisse aber behalte für dich – und denke, daß die Brosamen, die von der Tafel der Gottheit fallen, nicht für die Schweine sind, die im Kot wühlen.

Besorge auch nicht, daß du meine Geheimnisse vergessen wirst. Im Gegenteil, wenn du meinem Rath getreu bist, so wird dich der Engel des Lichts immer weiter führen.

Gebrauche alles nach der Vorschrift der Liebe, und findest du einen guten geprüften Menschen, so teile ihm so viel mit, als er ertragen kann – denn nicht alles was gut ist, ist auch jedem nutze – sagt Paulus.

•

Ich erbrach, las und erstaunte, ich warf mich zu Boden, und betete zu dem Gott der Liebe: *O, Gott, alle unsere Weisheit ist Torheit vor deinen Augen. Nur du allein, mein Gott, bist Wahrheit, bei dir allem will ich bleiben und nichts soll mich von dir mehr trennen. Amen!*

Einweihung.

Wenn du den Tag bestimmt hast, dich in die großen und heiligen Geheimnisse der Magie einzuweihen, so versammle einige Tage zuvor dein Gemüt, und denke über die große Wahrheit der Ewigkeit nach, bete zu Gott mit Zutrauen um Weisheit.

Sondere dich einige Tage von den Geschäften der Welt und den Menschen ab, und betrachte die Wichtigkeit der Einsamkeit und des Stillschweigens. Bestimme den Sonntag zu deiner Heiligung. Den Abend zuvor breite ein reines Tuch auf einer Wiese des Abends aus, und sammle am Morgen das Tau, das vom Himmel fällt. Gehe dann auf dein Zimmer, und richte den Altar zurecht, zünde die Wachskerzen an, und wiederhole das Gebet um Weisheit zu Gott. Wenn du dann gebetet hast, so entkleide dich, und wasche deinen Körper 7 mal mit einem frischen Wasser und sprich:

Du mein Gott! Laß mich den alten Menschen ausziehen, wie ich meine Kleider auszog, und laß meine Seele von den 7 Hauptlasten reinigen, wie ich meinen Körper 7 mal durch dieses Wasser reinige.

Wenn du dich so gewaschen hast, so wiederhole dein Gebet zu Gott. Reue, Erkenntnis, Glaube, Hoffnung und Liebe. Dann räuchere dich 7 mal und bitte zu Gott um die 7 Gaben des Geistes der Heiligung.

Das Rauchwerk besteht:

Sonntag.................Mastix

Montag.................Myrrhe

Dienstag................Aloe

Mittwoch...............Zimt

Donnerstag............Muskat

Freitag...................Safran

Samstag.................Cothus

(7) Nimm bei jeder Räucherung das Siegel und die Tabelle des Geistes in die Hand, und bitte Gott um diesen Grad der Heiligung. Dann wasche dich mit dem Tau des Himmels und sprich:

Heiliger Gott laß deinen Segen und deine Kraft über mich herabströmen, wie das Tau über die Blumen herabströmt, die du zu Zierde der Erde erhältst.

Dann kleide dich mit einem reinen, weißen Kleide an, das du durchgeräuchert hast, und sprich:

Mein Gott gib mir das Kleid der Unschuld, und wie ich dieses weiße Kleid anziehe, so will ich einen neuen Menschen anziehen, umgürte du mich mit deiner Weisheit und Gnade. Knie dann vor den Altar gegen Aufgang nieder und bete wie folgt:

1.

Heiliger Gott Eheieh! dessen Numeration Zepter, Krone und Diadem ist, der du durch die Ordnung der Seraphim einfließest, genannt Hayot Hakodesh, sende mir deine heilige Intelligenz Metatron, dessen Geschäft ist, die Engel vor deinen Antlitz zu führen, und durch den du mit Mose gesprochen hast, und erleuchte mich selben in den Angelegenheiten meines Leibes.

2.

Mächtiger Gott Tetragramaton Jod, dessen Numeration Chokmah Weisheit ist, der du deine Gewalt durch die Cherubim äußerst, Ophanim genannt, sende mir deine Weisheit vom Himmel herab, und laß deinen Engel Raziel, der der Führer Adams war, in jeder Angelegenheit meines Lebens, in welcher ich ihn durch deinen Heiligen Namen anrufe, zu meiner Hilfe und Erleuchtung an meiner Seele sein.

3.

Mächtiger Gott Tetragramaton Elohim, dessen Numeration Binah, oder Vorsicht und Einsicht ist, der du durch die Orden des Throne deinen Einfluss äußerst, Aralim genannt, schicke mir deinen heiligen Engel Zaphkiel, der der Führer Noe war, und deinen heiligen Engel Jophiel, der Führer Sem, und gib mir deutliche Erkenntnis meiner Sünden und Verzeihung, auch verleihe mir den Beistand dieser deiner Heiligen Engel in jeder dringenden Angelegenheit meines Lebens.

4.

Heiliger Gott El! dessen Numeration Chesed, oder Güte und Milde ist, der du durch die Ordnung der Herrschaften einfließt, genannt Chashmalim, schicke mir deinen Heiligen Engel Zadkiel, den Führer Abrahams, und gib mir Ruhe, Gerechtigkeit und Güte.

5.

Heiliger Gott Elohim Gibbor! dessen Numeration Geburah, oder Stärke und Kraft ist, der du durch die Ordnung der Gewalten einfliesst, genannt Seraphim, schicke mir deine heiligen Engel Camael, den Führer Simsons, und gib mir in den Angelegenheiten meines Lebens Stärke, Mut und Sieg.

6.

Heiliger Gott Eloha Vedaath, dessen Numeration Tiphareth, oder Zierde und Schönheit ist, der du durch die Ordnung der Tugend [Kräfte] genannt (8) Malachim deinen Einfluß äußerst, schicke mir deinen Heiligen Engel Raphael, den Führer Isaac und Tobias, deinen Heiligen Engel Peliel, den Führer Jakobs, und gib mir Leben, Tugend, Vergnügen und Schönheit.

7.

Heiliger Gott Tetragramaton Zebaoth oder Adonai Zebaoth, Gott der Heerscharen, dessen Numeration Netzach, oder Sieg und Triumph ist, der du durch die Fürsten, genannt Elohim, einfließt, schicke mir deinen Heiligen Haniel und Cerviel, den Führer Davids und gib mir Triumph über meine Leidenschaften, Sieg in meinen Angelegenheiten.

8.

Heiliger Gott Elohim Zebaoth! Gott der Heerscharen, dessen Numeration Hod ist, der durch die Ordnung der Erzengel einfließt, genannt Bene Elohim, schicke mir deinen Heiligen Engel Michael, den Führer Salomons, und lass mich in den Wissenschaften und Geheimnissen der Natur von ihm unterrichten.

9.

Heiliger Gott Sadai [der Allmächtige, sowie] Elchai [der lebendige Gott] – dessen Numeration Jesod ist, der du durch die Ordnung der Engel einfließt, genannt Cherubim – schicke mir deinen Heiligen Engel Gabriel, den Führer Josephs, Josua und Daniels, und gib mir, daß ich in deinen Heiligen Entsprechungen deinen Engeln Gehör gebe, und Folge leiste, auch laß mich durch sie vom Unglück bewahren und von künftigen Dingen benachrichtigen.

10.

Heiliger Gott Adonai Melech, Herr und König! Dessen Numeration Malkuth ist, der du durch die Ordnung der Heiligen Seelen einfließt, genannt Issim, oder Heroen und Fürsten, schicke mir deine Heilige Intelligenz Metatron, und gib mir durch sie die Gabe der Prophezeiung, der Wunder und der Wissenschaften der Propheten.

•

Wenn du diese Gebete vollendet hast, so nehme die 7 Sigillen der Engel, und netze sie mit dem Tau des Himmels und räuchere jedes mit dem Rauch, der ihm gehört.

Dann nimm von Saiden die 7 Farben des Regenbogens, und vermache jedes Sigill, und drücke dein Siegel der Liebe darauf mit dem Gebet:

Gebet.

Ihr heiligen Engel Cherubim, Seraphim, Heerscharen, Mächte und Fürsten ich beschwöre euch durch den Heiligen Gott, versaget mir in keiner Angelegenheit meines Lebens euren Beistand, und versprecht der Gegenwart des Allmächtigen in jedem Fall eure Hilfe und Unterstützung, wie ich euch entgegen verspreche, euren Einsprechenden allzeit Gehör zu geben, und mich eures Beistandes nicht unwürdig zu machen, führt mich zur göttlichen Weisheit, und zum höchsten Glück unserer Bestimmung.

Ich schließe mit euch nach dem Willen und Absichten des heiligen Gottes, den ihr anbetet, den Bund der Liebe, und verspreche und gelobe nach meinen Kräften alles zu erfüllen, was die Liebe gegen (10) Gott und gegen meinen Nächsten von mir erfordert, zum Zeichen unserer Vereinigung und eures mir geweihten Beistandes, siegle ich 7 Sigillen mit dem Siegel der Liebe. Amen.

Nach diesem Gebet nimm den Ring der 7 Engel, wasche ihn mit dem Tau, und räuchere ihn mit dem Rauch der Sieben, dann sprich:

Dieser Ring sei der Bund der Vereinigung zwischen mir und den heiligen Engeln der Gottheit. Er diene zum Schutz in allen Gefahren und zum ewigen Denkmal der himmlischen Verbindung.

Alsdann kleide dich vollkommen an, und nimm 3 Bänder, ein weißes, ein rosenrothes und himmelblaues, und binde sie an einander und sprich: *Mein Gott! gib mir deine Gnade, daß ich mein körperliches, sichtliches und geistiges Leben nach deinen heiligen Absichten verbinde und der großen Gnade der Heiligung würdig werden möchte.*

Verbrenne dann dieses Band und sprich: *Wie keine Menschenhand diesen Bund gelöst hat, so löse auch keine irdische Macht mehr meinen Bund mit Gott und den Engeln.*

Wenn du dieses gebetet hast, so nehme das schwarze Band und zerreiße es und sprich:

Wie ich dies schwarze Band zerreiße, so sei von dieser Stunde das Band zerrissen, das mich an die Finsternissen und Welt kettete; ich schwöre daher den Fürsten der Finsternissen der Welt und ihren Gelüsten und dem Fleisch auf ewig ab.

Verbrenne dann dieses Band, und binde ein weißes Band um deine Stirne und sprich:

Mein Gott! reinige meine Seele, und verbinde mich mit dem Band der Unschuld mit deinen heiligen Engeln.

Dann entzünde den Opfer-Altar, und sprich: *Alles ist eitel, ausgenommen Gott allein lieben und ihm dienen.*

Zerstöre dann den Altar, und sprich: *Von nun an sei mein Herz Gottes Tempel, und mein Altar meine Liebe. Amen.*

•

F. Wo kommst du her?

Antw. Von Bensalem.

F. Wo liegt der Ort?

Antw. Gegen Orient abgesondert von den Menschen.

F. Warum gegen Orient?

Antw. Weil das Licht vom Anfang kommt.

F. Ist es Tag in Bensalem?

Antw. Die Sonne steht am Hohen Mittag.

F. Wird es Nacht in Bensalem?

Antw. Nein – denn die Sonne leuchtet immer im Mittelpunkt.

F. Steht ein Tempel in Bensalem?

Antw. Dem Herzen des Menschen ist kein Tempel da.

F. Wie heißt die Hinschrift?

Antw. Wahrheit und Güte.

F. Was war mein Geschäft in Bensalem?

Antw. Den alten Menschen abzulegen und wiedergeboren zu werden. [11]

F. Erkläre mir das Wort Bensalem.

Antw. Es ist die Progression des 1 – zu 2 – und jeder Buchstabe hat daher 2 Auslegung.

1.

Bene agere

exigere Miseros

Negligere Nihil

salutem aeternitatis quaerere

Amare omnes

Laborare pro Humanitate, Deo et patria

Exigere nullum pretium

Mundana contemnere

2.

Bene volens esse

Errores corrigere

nauseare fastum et voluptates

sobri esse et costus

arma ferre pro patria et principe

legibus se subjecere

Exemplum esse virtutis

Mortem non trepidare

Worin besteht das große Geheimnis?

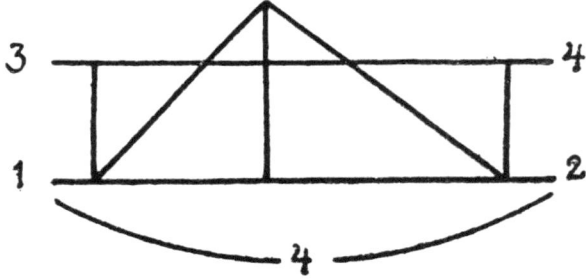

Chapter 4.

Bernhard Schleiß von Löwenfeld: The highest Symbolic Grade of Magic. A manuscript left behind by a wise man to his son.

[1] In 1774, on the twenty-eighth of June, my father gave me a sealed parcel with the following inscription: My son, do not open this parcel earlier than in the thirty-third year of your age upon your birthday – I instruct you to do so according to the obedience you owe me,. Were you to open it earlier against my will, all my good intentions, with which I present these papers to you, would be thwarted. But if you are obedient and fulfil my command, God will bless you and my purpose shall be achieved.

So take this parcel, and seal it in the iron box I gave you, and place the herbs next to it as I have instructed, and bury this box by the big oak tree in the Breitwald, adjacent to the church on the hill where we often used to sit. Bury it three feet deep, and every year inspect it and refresh the herbs, which you are aware of, that it will not rot.

I order you to do this so that these papers will not fall into the hands of an unworthy person. He would not understand the secrets because he does not know the cipher – but it is better if it does not happen at all.

Take this gift, dear son, on your twenty-second birthday, and if I live not to see the joy of wishing you happiness on your thirty-third birthday, then open the parcel and accept my blessing in that world by an invisible hand.

In the year 1785, the twenty-eighth of June, I had my box, which I had visited annually, opened it and found in it the following text, beside a second parcel that was sealed again.

•

My son! You are now at the age of manhood, and if you have been faithful to my teachings which I gave you in your youth, you will be worthy of the greater mysteries which I will teach you. From your youth you have had joy in strange and fantastical things; but you were not yet at an age mature enough to become acquainted with the higher secrets of nature, so I had to save my teaching until your more mature age, and so I gave you these papers; if I should live no longer, know ye they will teach you well.

Alongside the package you now open, you will find another one, do not open the latter until you have read what is written herein, I implore you, for it would bring you to ruin.

Before you continue reading, bow down thy head before the Infinite and pray:

Prayer.

You God of my fathers, and most merciful Lord! You, who created all things by your word. [2] And by thy wisdom hast ordained that man shall reign over the natures created by thee, that he shall also rule the world with equity and righteousness, and judge with sincerity of heart.

Grant me the wisdom which stands before thy throne, and cast me not away from the number of thy servants.

For I am your servant, a son of your handmaid, and a weak man; I can do nothing without you, and without your divine wisdom all the wisdom of men is folly in your eyes.

Send me then the wisdom from your holy heavens, and from the throne of your sovereignty, that it may always be with me, working with me, that I may know what is pleasing to you. Amen.

Now when you have finished this prayer, read on:

I was, my son, of the society of those who seek wisdom. Our motto was: Truth and Mercy: our number 75. Our secret word: Vaudahat. Our nomination Thiphareth. The rest the sealed package will explain.

The symbol of our remembrance is four hearts, concentrated in the centre and forming the shape of a cross, bound by chains into a unified whole.

This symbol is the sign that should constantly remind us of the high duties of the human endeavor, as I will now explain.

Our Society, dear son, has no bond with any society that has ever existed, or that may exist. We are not bound by oaths – we hold no constitutions or written rules, we keep no convents or lodges. Our work is the active love of God and man – our order is the order of God, of the saints, of magic, and of the wise.

We do not accept anyone; everyone accepts himself according to the degree of love he gives himself through his actions, and according to this he transfers himself into the higher or lower degree of Divine Approximation.

We have no superiors; we are all equal among ourselves – our directorate is God.

We need neither secretary nor seal keeper; the angel who enters the good deeds of men in the book of eternity is our secretary, and the only seal we acknowledge is the stamp of the purest intention, which prints the seal of love upon our actions.

No one of us commands the other; each commands himself according to the degree of his knowledge.

We exclude no one; each excludes himself by the degree to which he descends when he leaves Truth and Mercy. We do not form a state within a state, but we are good people among people.

[3] There are no ceremonies with us; our initiation is active love of God and man.

We teach each other without seeing each other, we know each other through active love, and according to the purity of love one shows, each one can tell the degree of wisdom possessed by the other.

Honours, precedence and special merits are nothing to us; they are signs of the still uneducated work in the temple of God. The master builder alone determines our value; we cannot assume merit for ourselves, nor determine the degree of merit of our brothers.

The true Mason's lodges (but they are few) are planting schools, from which man emerges when he comes to gnosis [Erkenntnis], that is to higher wisdom, then he comes from the material into the spiritual, or from the visible into the invisible.

Only the young man, who is also not a Mason, can reach this degree of height because if his will is good, God leads him to wisdom.

Since material man could seldom think his way into such great truths, our ancestors believed that sensual man could gradually be formed into non-sensual man, and therefore they concealed the truth of great mysteries in figures to gradually lead man to knowledge, and thus masonry came into being.

But the polished stone, which yearns to tell the truth, soon showed crevices because people degenerated and made false intentions for their purposes and the truth became lost in ceremonies.

Unfortunately, that is still how most of the Masons's lodges remain today: they promise to lead people to the light, and yet themselves do grope in darkness.

So beware my son! And do not let the outward appearance blind your eye, but follow my advice, and wisdom shall receive you into her bosom.

The highest degree of wisdom knows no ceremony – the angels closest to the Godhead are naked; the garment is the sign of our knowledge of our nakedness.

I will lead you to the highest level of the temple – I will show you the truth in its light, and I will tear away the emblematic curtain from its sanctum, which hitherto covered it in front of your more foolish eyes because you might not have been able to bear its light.

Learn my son to cultivate the highest levels of man's happiness, this happiness is the true in knowledge and the good in practice, and meanwhile enjoy the benefits that the true and good grant to you.

Receive the final symbol of the highest degree of magic, which shall be an eternal reminder of your highest duties, which I will now explain to you.

[4] You are now passing into the company of the wise; at that moment when your will is firm and your love pure, you are connected with them, and an angel whom Wisdom sends to lead you will be your guide; never make yourself unworthy of his presence. You will recall that we have neither ceremonies nor temple; our temple is the world, our ceremonies are the practice of the works of love.

Our work is the true and the good, and the marriage of Truth and Mercy is wisdom; our highest Master is God, our co-workers are angels and the wise.

Our bond is the bond of love that unites man with man, and man with angels and God.

My son! Alike is chained to alike, similar to similar, you shall be connected with your alike, with your similar, according to the degree of your love.

Without knowing how, you will become acquainted with people of high nature, for neither salvation nor death separates the wise man from the wise, because for him there is neither space nor time.

The more your spirituality opens you up, the more you will receive supernatural knowledge; you will be guided by exalted beings.

In the society you are now entering, you can neither cheat nor be cheated, where there is truth the false cannot stand the test, and pretence cannot stand the test.

The society of the wise is the account that separates the chaff from the grain.

It is a house in which the evil one cannot dwell.

You shut yourself out again when you become contemptible – when you move away from the light. It is again your fault when blindness darkens the eyes of your soul.

Walk with courage and confidence. An invisible being will guide you – the greatest secrets of nature, miracles, healing will be your part. Wisdom grants these gifts, and I bid you to receive them without envy, without resentment.

I now explain to you, my son, the supreme symbol.

•

This symbol consists of four hearts, chained one to other. In the middle is a radiant sphere with the inscription *The True*. On the other side is written: *The Good*. The four hearts form the square of love, through which everything exists.

Love God – your prince and your fatherland, the people, your brothers, and your enemies.

Love God without self-love, love your prince and your fatherland without self-interest, the people your brothers, without intention of reward, and your enemies without hope that they will ever become your friends. These additions characterise the highest degree of love, and make us more alike the Godhead.

[5] *The front and reverse images*.

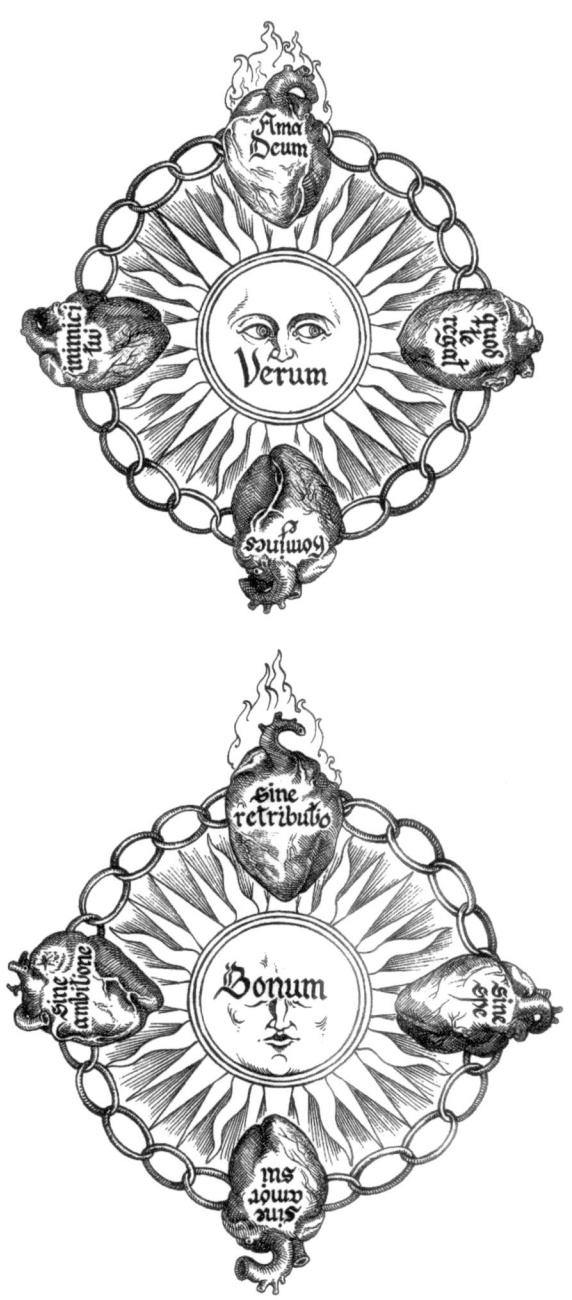

The pure gold of which this emblem is made symbolizes purity of soul, for which all men should strive.

The polish is the sign that one should cleanse oneself of all blemishes that prevent one from receiving the light of the eternal sun.

As the four hearts on the chain symbolize love, the centre means the Godhead, the first of all good things – from which everything comes, where everything is aimed.

The number four means the duration of the permanence of things: The number IV is the magic of being, of existence, of deeds, it is the balance of nature, according to which everything weighs itself. So take this sign, my son, from your father's hand, and bind it to your side with a band of fire-coloured ribbon, and wear it as a constant reminder of your duties.

The colour of the ribbon reminds you that your zeal shall never cool, alike to the fire of your love.

Purify your heart, gather your soul, choose solitude, and pray to God – and make yourself worthy to receive the highest degree of the holy magic.

Let the above symbol be placed in a seal with the inscription *totum unitur amore* (from love it unites), and if you are in correspondence with a good man, he will know you, but do not forget to press the seal of true love in every one of your actions – for what would the symbol be without truth?

Now open the second package, and from it learn the way to the great secrets according to the cipher which I did not teach you; you can read it for yourself; if you have read it, so burn all my papers, and only keep the holy secrets in your heart.

[6] But you can copy this my introduction, even if you find it suitable according to your time to communicate to the lovers of truth, to give them healthy notions of true wisdom. But keep the secrets to yourself, and think that the crumbs that fall from the table of the Godhead are not for the pigs that rummage in the dung.

Also, do not worry that you will forget my secrets. On the contrary, if you are faithful to my counsel, the angel of light will always lead you further.

Use everything according to the rules of love, and if you find a good, tested person, tell him as much as he can bear – because not everything that is good is also good for everyone, says Paul.

•

I opened, read and was amazed, I threw myself to the ground and prayed to the God of love: *O, God, all our wisdom is folly in thy sight. Only you alone, my God, are truth, with you I want to remain and nothing shall separate me from you. Amen!*

•

Initiation.

When you have chosen the day to initiate yourself into the great and holy mysteries of magic, gather your mind a few days before and reflect on the great truth of eternity. Pray to God with confidence for wisdom.

Separate yourself for a few days from the affairs of the world and other people, and consider the importance of solitude and silence.

Decide on a Sunday for your sanctification. The evening before, spread a pure cloth in a meadow of the evening, and in the morning, collect the dew that falls from the sky.

Then go to your room and prepare the altar, light the wax candles and repeat the prayer for wisdom to God. When you have prayed then, undress and wash your body seven times with fresh water and speak:

You my God! Let me take off the old man as I took off my clothes, and let my soul be cleansed of the 7 major burdens as I cleanse my body 7 times with this water.

If you have washed in this manner, repeat the prayer to God. Repentance, knowledge, faith, hope and love. Then burn incense 7 times and ask God for the 7 gifts of the Spirit of Sanctification.

The incense consists of:

Sunday.................Mastic

Monday...............Myrrh

Tuesday................Aloe

Wednesday...........Cinnamon

Thursday..............Nutmeg

Friday...................Saffron

Saturday................Costus [*Costus speciosus* or *Saussurea costus*]

[7] With the burning of each incense take the seal and table of the spirit in your hand, and ask God for the respective degree of sanctification. Then wash yourself with the dew of heaven and speak:

Holy God let your blessing and your power descend upon me as the dew descends upon the flowers, which you sustain for the adornment of the earth.

Then put on a pure white dress, which you have thoroughly exposed to the smoke, and speak:

My God give me the garment of innocence, and as I put on this white garment, I put on a new man, and you gird me with your wisdom and grace.
Then kneel before the altar at the entrance to the temple and pray as follows[19]:

1.

Holy God Eheieh! whose number is Sceptre, Crown and Diadem, who streams in through the order of Seraphim, called Hayot Hakodesh, send me your holy intelligence Metatron, whose duty is to bring the angels before your

---

19 in the following, see Agrippa of Nettesheim, *De Occulta Philosophia*, Book 3, Chapter X; sephiroth and angel names corrected by Frater Acher

countenance, and through whom you spoke with Moses, and enlighten me the same in the affairs of my body.

2.

Mighty God Tetragramaton Yod, whose number is Chokmah, wisdom, you who exercise your power through the Cherubim, called Ophanim, send me your wisdom from heaven, and let your angel Raziel, who was the leader to Adam, be at my aid in all matters of my life, in which I call upon him through your holy name, to grant me help and the enlightenment of my soul.

3.

Mighty God Tetragramaton Elohim, whose number is Binah, or Prudence and Insight, who through the Orders of the Throne exalts your influence, called Aralim, send me your Holy Angel Zaphkiel, who was the leader of Noah, and your Holy Angel Jophiel, the leader of Shem, and give me clear knowledge of my sins and forgiveness, and also grant me the assistance of these, your Holy Angels in every urgent matter of my life.

4.

Holy God El! whose number is Chesed, or Goodness and Mercy, you, who stream in through the Order of Dominions, called Chashmalim, send me your Holy Angel Zadkiel, the leader of Abraham, and give me peace, justice and goodness.

5.

Holy God, Elohim Gibbor, whose number is Geburah, or Strength and Power, you, who flow in through the Order of Powers, called Seraphim, send me your holy angel, Camael, the leader of Simson, and give me strength, courage and victory in the affairs of my life.

6.

Holy God Eloha Vedaath, whose number is Tiphareth, or Ornament and Beauty, you, who exert your influence through the Order of Virtue [Forces],[8] called Malachim, send me your Holy Angel Raphael, leader of Isaac and Tobias, your Holy Angel Peliel, the leader of Jacob, and give me life, virtue, pleasure and beauty.

7.

Holy God Tetragramaton Zebaoth or Adonai Zebaoth, God of Hosts, whose number is Netzach, or Victory and Triumph, you, who stream in through the princes, called Elohim, send me your holy Haniel and Cerviel, the leader of David and grant me triumph over my passions, victory in my affairs.

8.

Holy God Elohim Zebaoth! God of Hosts, whose number is Hod, you, who flow in through the Order of Archangels, called Bene Elohim, send me your Holy Angel Michael, the Leader of Solomon, and let me learn from him in the sciences and mysteries of nature.

9.

Holy God Sadai [the Almighty, as well as] ElChai [the Living God] – whose number is Yesod, you, who stream in through the order of Angels, called Cherubim – send me your Holy Angel Gabriel, the leader of Joseph, Joshua and Daniel, and grant me that through your Holy Correspondences I may grant hearing to your angels and obey them, and through them let me keep from misfortune and be warned of future things.

10.

Holy God Adonai Melek, Lord and King! Whose number is Malkuth, you who enter through the Order of the Holy Souls, called Issim, or Heroes and Princes, send me your Holy Intelligence Metatron, and grant me through it the gift of prophecy, miracles and the sciences of the prophets.

When you have finished these prayers, take the seven sigils of the angels and net them with the dew of heaven and fumigate each one with the smoke that belongs to it.

Then take from silk the 7 colours of the rainbow, and bequeath each sigil, and put your seal of love on it with the following prayer:

Prayer.

Holy Angels, Cherubim, Seraphim, Hosts, Powers and Princes, I beseech you by the Holy God, do not fail to give me your assistance in any matter of my life, and promise your help and support to the presence of the Almighty in any case, just as I promise to listen to your inspiration and prompts at all times and not to make myself unworthy of your assistance, lead me towards divine wisdom and to the supreme happiness of our destiny.

I enter with you, according to the will and intentions of the Holy God whom you worship, into the Covenant of Love, and I promise and vow, to the best of my ability, to fulfil all that love that

[10] *God and my neighbour require of me; as a sign of our union and your consecrated assistance, I seal 7 sigils with the seal of love. Amen.*

After this prayer, take the ring of the seven angels, wash it with the dew, and pass it through the smoke of the seven, then speak:

Let this ring be the bond of union between me and the Holy Angels of the Godhead. It shall serve as a safeguard in all dangers and as an everlasting memorial of the heavenly union.

Then dress yourself completely and take three ribbons, one white, one rose-red and one sky-blue, and bind them together and say: *My God! Grant me your grace that I may unite my physical, visible and spiritual life according to your holy intentions and become worthy of the great grace of sanctification.* Then burn this ribbon and say: *As no human hand has broken this covenant, so no earthly power can break my covenant with God and the Angels.*

When you have prayed this, take the black ribbon and tear it and speak: *As I tear this black ribbon, so shall be torn from this hour the bond that chained me to the darknesses and this world; I hereby renounce for ever the lords of the darknesses of the world and their lusts and the flesh.*

Then burn this ribbon and tie a white ribbon around your forehead and speak:

My God! Purify my soul and bind me with the bond of innocence with your Holy Angels.

Then light the altar of sacrifice and say: *Everything is vain except loving and serving God alone.*

Then destroy the altar, and say: *From now on my heart shall be the temple of God, and my altar [shall be] my love. Amen.*

•

Q. Where are you from?

Answ. From Bensalem.

Q. Where is this place?

Answ. In the orient, apart from the people.

Q. Why in the orient [East]?

Answ. Because the light comes from the beginning.

Q. Is it daytime in Bensalem?

Answ. The sun is at high-noon.

Q. Is it night in Bensalem?

Answ. No - because the sun always shines in the centre.

Q. Is there a temple in Bensalem?

Answ. There is no temple in the heart of man.

Q. What is the inscription?

Answ. Truth and Goodness.

Q. What was my business in Bensalem?

Answ. To cast off the old man and be born again. [11]

Q. Explain the word Bensalem to me.

Answ. It is the progression of 1 to 2 and therefore each letter has 2 interpretations.

1.

bene agere [do good]

exigere miseros [dispel misery]

negligere nihil [neglect nothing]

salutem aeternitatis quaerere [search salvation in eternity]

amare omnes [love everyone]

laborare pro humanitate, Deo et patria [work for humanity, God and the country]

exigere nullum pretium [levy no money]

mundana contemnere [disdain mundane matters]

2.

bene volens esse [strive to be good]

errores corrigere [correct errors]

nauseare fastum et voluptates [sicken at arrogance and carnal pleasures]

sobri esse et costus [be sober and 'costus']

arma ferre pro patria et principe [go to war for country and prince]

legibus se subjecere [subject to the law]

exemplar esse virtutis [be an example of virtues]

mortem non trepidare [not to fear death]

What is the great secret?

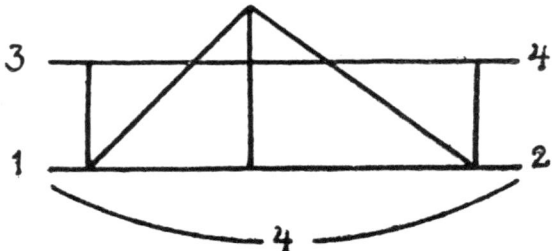

Chapter 5.

The highest Symbolic Grade of Magic – A Ritual Analysis

The document we reprinted here in its original German form in Chapter 3 and in its full English translation in Chapter 4 presents itself as a magical testament from father to son. Rather than wealth and possessions what is passed on is a pathway towards divine communion in the form of precise instructions on how to create a personal angelic covenant.

The father didn't write the text on his deathbed, but with clear foresight and intention – handing it over to his son on his 22nd birthday, and asking him to keep it buried and looked after for eleven years, until his 33rd birthday, when he would be deemed ready to absorb the deep mysteries it contains.

Just like the son, who after more than a decade of waiting unearthed the instructions to self-initiate into the *Highest Degree of Magic*, so this testament reaches us today. Some two-hundred fifty years from when it was first handed over, unless of course the opening paragraphs are part of a literary artifice by the author, we open this parcel again.

And just as it were when the pages lay in the hands of the son, so it is now with us: What we make of it, is entirely up to us.

A map towards the angelic mysteries has been placed into our hands. Whether or not we choose to walk the path it shows, no father or other authority ever can decide for us; they can only hope that we encounter the text when we are ready for what it has to offer.

1. Origins

Obviously, the literary introduction to the text is reminiscent of one of the most famous texts of Western Magic and in particular of the art of creating angelic covenant, *The Sacred Magic of Abramelin the Mage (Das Buch der wahren Praktik der göttlichen Magie).*

Here also the reader is introduced to the magical instructions contained in the text by an autobiographical introduction from father to son.

Specifically, the father takes the same precautions by writing the text long before his last hour, then placing it into a chest and locking it up, to ensure that text and younger son will only encounter each other when the latter is a fully grown man and ready to understand the mysteries hinted at within it.

> *This is the book of the true practice of Magical Wisdom. It has been passed to me – Abraham, the son of Simon, son of Juda, the son of Simon – by oral tradition [...] I have written this manuscript and placed it in a chest so that my houngest son, Lamech, will have a special treasure as his inheritance.*[20]

This brings us to the question of authorship, and whether we can presume our current author had been familiar with the Abramelin-tradition, thus deliberately copying the introductory remarks to strengthen the ties of their own material to this authoritative magical text.

Just as the transmission of the text itself so also our best lead to identifying its author stems from the well-known German Freemason, Dr. Bernhard Beyer (1879-1966). Beyer worked as a head neurologist of a large clinic, while also being a highly active and public proponent of Freemasonry, in particular of the tradition of humanitarian Freemasonry.

---

20 Abraham von Worms, after Dehn, 2015, p. 3

He was a member and grandmaster of several lodges and founded the *Museum of Freemasonry* in Bayreuth/Germany as well as the *Historic League* (*Geschichtlicher Engbund*), dedicated to objective research into the history of Freemasonry. He also played a central role in reviving Freemasonry in Germany in the 1950s, after the Second World War.

Beyer's most prominent literary contributions remain his in-depth study of the history, rituals and doctrines of the Order of the Golden and Rosy Cross[21], as well as his editorial activity for the seven volumes of occult documents compiled in the *The Freemason's Museum*.[22]

It is in the fifth volume of the *Museum* that Beyer published our current text (pp. 215). Specifically, he positions it as an addendum to his book on the Order of the Golden and Rosy Cross (OGR). Here is a translation of the short preamble offered by Beyer, where he shines a light on the origins of our document:

> *In the first volume of our "Freemason's Museum", as part of my work on the "Doctrines of the Order of the Golden and Rosy Cross" (p.250) I referred to a document in the [Georg Burkhard] Kloß' archive, which might grant insights on the degree of the mage [Magus-Grad] of the mentioned order. Meanwhile, thanks to the kindness of the Great-Orient of the Netherlands, I was able to review this document and determine that it does not correspond to the previously raised expectations. However, it remains without a doubt that it emerged from the circles of the Order of the Golden and Rosy Cross; equally I am still convinced that its author was Bernh. Jos. Schleiß von Löwenfeld. As in addition it contains some wonderful things and as it especially makes for an important supplement to the portrait of the order, I shall transcribe it here in its original form.*[23]

---

21 Bernhard Beyer, *Das Lehrsystem des Ordens der Gold- und Rosenkreuzer*, Leipzig: Pansophie Verlag, 1925

22 *Das Freimaurer-Museum*. Band 1-7. Archiv für freimaurerische Ritual-Kunde und Geschichts-Forschung. In zwangloser Folge herausgegeben vom Geschichtlichen Engbund des Bayreuther Freimaurer-Museums. Handschrift für Brr Meister, 1925-1931

23 Beyer, 1930, p.217

113

Beyer thus informs us that the instructions on their final grade as a mage remained missing from the vast amount of material he could gather in internal archives of the Order of the Golden and Rosy Cross. The very manuscript which he had hoped would fill this remaining gap turned out to be something different: An ostensibly personal document by one of the founding fathers of the order, written as a magical testament to his son.

Bernhard Joseph Schleiß von Löwenfeld (1731-1800) was a court and medical counsellor in the German Electoral Palatinate (*Kurpfalz*), a city doctor of Sulzbach and, more relevant to our study, the author of two well-known Rosicrucian books, published under pseudonym, as well as a significant member of the Order of the Golden and Rosy Cross who had been involved in their original founding.[24]

He is particularly remembered today for his 1782 book, published under his lodge name *Phoebron*, and titled *The Rosicrucian radiating in the Light of Truth*.[25] Schleiß's position in the order at the time of the publication of this book remains obscure, as we have evidence indicating his "secret exclusion" before the year 1788, i.e. possibly indicating not a formal exclusion, but a passive connivance due to his original significant role for the order and already advanced age.[26]

Despite his ambiguous position in the order, Schleiß seems to have been determined to both write and release this book under immense time pressure. For it formed a rather polemic apology directed against Hans Karl von Ecker und Eckhoffen's 1781 now famous pasquil *The Rosicrucian in their Nakedness*.[27] Although Pianco, aka von Ecker had asked the order to issue a personal response to his book, Schleiß's

---

24 Geffarth, 2007, p.167

25 *Der im Lichte der Wahrheit strahlende Rosenkreutzer*, Leipzig, Christian Gottlieb Hilscher, 1782

26 Geffarth, 2007, p.167

27 *Der Rosenkreuzer in seiner Blösse: Zum Nutzen der Staaten hingestellt durch Zweifel wider die wahre Weisheit der so genannten ächten Freymäurer oder goldnen Rosenkreutzer des alten Systems, von Magister Pianco, vieler Kreisen Bundsverwandten*, Amsterdam, Nürnberg, 1781

rushed apology was at best tolerated, but certainly not welcome by the order. It was an obvious rule that an occult order would never react publicly to any public allegations or accusations such as those made by their former member Hans Karl von Ecker.[28]

In light of such historic context, and returning to our original text, we find ourselves presented with several paradoxes: Von Ecker's book was meant as an open attack to discredit the Order of the Golden and Rosy Cross, as he intended to create space and credibility for his own newly founded order, the *Asiatic Brethren*.[29]

On the other side of the dispute we find Schleiß von Löwenfeld attempting to distinguish himself as the public defender of the original order; yet he does so without their mandate, possibly already being excluded or at least stripped bare of any internal position of power.

This picture is now further complicated by the actual content of the document at hand: Dated to 1774, i.e. five years before Schleiß's public defence of the Order of the Golden and Rosy Cross, the author reveals himself as a member of a secret covenant of wise men which is explicitly different from the Order of the Golden and Rosy Cross. Specifically, the author stresses:

> *Our Society, dear son, has no bond with any society that has ever existed, or that may exist – we are not bound by oaths – we have no constitutions or written rules, no convents or lodges, our work is the active love of God and man – our order is the order of God – of the saints – of magic – of the wise.* (p. 2)

Here we hear the voice of an elder who has lost all illusions of ancient lineages and occult orders, as far as their outer man-made representations are concerned. In many regards he paints the picture of the precise opposite of what the Order of the Golden and Rosy Cross had become: A society so rigid and hierarchical, Renko Geffarth in his extensive 2007 study chose it as the prime example of a once secret society turning into a full-blown secret church.

28 Geffarth, 2007, p.167
29 For further reference see Acher, 2015

Two possible options present themselves to resolve this paradox: Either we have to consider Beyer might have been wrong in attributing our present manuscript to Bernhard Schleiß von Löwenfeld, and indeed we are reading the lines of an altogether different contemporary of the second half of the 18th century. Or alternatively, in the present document we hear the voice of Schleiß during a time when he was particularly disenfranchised with the Order of the Golden and Rosy Cross – possibly during the days of his disempowerment while the order was going through one of its many reforms. In this latter case it would be of no surprise to find Schleiß taking such a sharp stance against the flaws of all man-made occult organisations, and guiding his son (or magical heir?) towards a more direct mystical path of creating an angelic covenant through self-initiation. This scenario would have still allowed Schleiß to defend 'his' order against the defamation publicly agitated by von Ecker five years later. Maybe Schleiß would have even done so with heightened verve and delight, as the old man by then was pushed onto the periphery of an order he had once co-founded, and releasing this book against the preference of the current order-heads might have been his only way of raising his voice again.

Be that as it may, after many lengthy chapters in Schleiß's apology about the allegedly true history of the Rosicrucians (e.g. most notably the mentioning of the ancient Order of the *Ormusen* or *Wise of the Light* (*Lichtweisen*), as a group in the first century CE that transferred Egyptian mystery knowledge into Christianity), we finally hear him reaffirm a similarly subversive tone as the author of our present document: He states the explicit notion that in the end the entire wisdom of the Rosicrucian order does not stem from human transmission, but from personal contact with the Divine Spirit.

> *Just like the true ancient wise, so the true Rosicrucians received their constitution, teachings, sciences, all their tables and their entire laws through the degrees of the illuminated influence of the spirit of divine wisdom.*[30]

---

30 Phoebron, 1782, p.223

Were we to follow the lead of Schleiß von Löwenfeld as the author of our manuscript, we could positively resolve the question posed above: As a founding member of the OGR Schleiß would have had access to extensive occult archives and collections of his time. The first German print edition of the Abramelin text was published in 1725 by Peter Hammer; thus, if not through earlier manuscript forms, we have to presume Schleiß's familiarity with the printed version of the *Book of True Practice*.

However, this in return highlights another problematic aspect of our text. The then only extant copy was published by Beyer in the fifth volume of his *Freimaurer-Museum*. Yet despite both Schleiß's and Beyer's extensive occult knowledge many of the Hebrew divine and angelic names appear in garbled forms. Possible explanations could be that Beyer worked in haste while doing his transcript in the *Bibliotheca Klossiana* where he encountered the original document; or alternatively, he might not have copied his version from the original Schleiß manuscript, but from another earlier transcript. After all, we have no leads as to how such a seemingly private document, handed down from father to son in a double-sealed package, ended up in the famous occult library and archive of Georg Burkhard Kloß (1787-1854).

In conclusion, it is not unusual with occult ritual texts that their origins can remain more occult than their actual content. While we can illumine the latter through our practice, we must stand in the meandering stream of secrecy, myth and reality in regard to the former. For our current manuscript this means we won't be able to tell if its literary appearance as a testament is a romantic homage to Abramelin or the authentic magical legacy of Schleiß von Löwenfeld to his son. What we do know, though, is that the text emerged from the 18th century occult milieu of the OGR and the early *Asiatic Brethren*. And yet it depicts a rather anti-authoritarian, self-empowering current of angelic magic.

Finally, given that it presents itself as an initiation into the highest degree of magic, it could also be read as a natural progression: From more closely guided and guarded magical development in the lower ranks of a magical order, towards the final step on the rung: Realising that the man-made aspects of any secret society are only outer dressings, and stepping into angelic covenant all by oneself.

2. General Instructions

Our text is structured in three distinct phases: The first phase consists of the opening sequence and short introduction (p. 1) where the reader hears the initial account of how the son has come into possession of the documents and cared for their secret preservation for eleven years.

The second phase (p. 1-6) begins with the opening of the first parcel on 28th of June 1785. Now the reader takes the position of the son, is introduced to the voice of the father and given general instructions about the society of wise men. The third and final phase consists of the ritual instructions (p. 6-11).

The voice of the father insists that this sequence of familiarising oneself with the given material is of critical importance. Specifically, such warning points to the importance of the second phase, and ensuring to keep the ritual instructions *sealed* until all aspects of the general instructions have been absorbed and brought to life in one's own practice. As we have exemplified in *Black Abbot · White Magic* it is a common trait of many magical texts to hide critical messages in their periphery; i.e. to direct superficial attention away from their actual keys and towards something more shiny and sparkling placed in their seeming centre (e.g. seals, invocations, ritual formulas).

In some cases the reader will need to bring both parts together, the keys hidden in the textual periphery and the overtly ritualistic instructions, to ensure magical efficacy. In other cases the keys hidden in periphery present the actual message alone, and the central rituals or seals are nothing but outer dressings to protect the mysteries.

The magical relevance of the general instructions are further highlighted when the reader is asked to speak a prayer before reading them. As part of this first prayer we are given a critical key, easy to overlook by the cursory reader:

> [...] *And by thy wisdom hast ordained that man shall reign over the natures* [sic!] *created by thee, that he shall also rule the world with equity and righteousness, and judge with sincerity of heart.* (p. 2)

In rather explicit terms we are introduced to the general tenet that without perfecting the three virtues of equity, righteousness and sincerity of heart, no magical progress shall be expected. These human qualities are not mentioned as empty words, but they are presented as the essential tools determined by divine wisdom for man to reign over the multiple natures (sic!) of creation.

So, in case you are reading this as a magical practitioner yourself, we put this question in front of you even more overtly: What do these three virtues mean to you personally? What do you see as their benefits, and what as their pitfalls? What does great look like for each one of these, if perfected in your own life? And how would others know that you have progressed in your work on them?

These are the kind of personal reflections meant to be triggered by the first prayer. For speaking to Divinity about the qualities that enable man to reign over creation by definition should be a humbling experience. For who are we, in our flawed human state, to strut such flawless qualities?

This also speaks to the particular kind of magic illustrated in this document: Other type of spirits might ask for a golden ring or a cup of blood offered during the hour of the Moon. Speaking comparatively, such material offerings are easy to come by. The spirits we are dealing with here are asking for a much more essential kind of offering. Here, the practitioner themselves becomes the cup that has to be filled with divine qualities so the spirits can commune with them. Thus, the ego of the practitioner becomes the sacrifice – offering up the vast space it used to dominate to virtues directly connected to the angelic realm. Such is the essential precondition for the practitioner to become alike to the angelic realm. And this is precisely what we find expressed in the third paragraph of the initial prayer: The request to Divinity to be granted the same privilege as the most ascended angels, standing upright in front of the throne, seeing Divinity eye to eye and being able to be present at the threshold of the abyss.

> *Grant me the wisdom which stands before thy throne, and cast me not away from the number of thy servants.* (p. 2)

The result of such kind of magic is not a single event, but a lasting transformation of the practitioner. Angelic communion in this sense is both a moment in time, a specific encounter, as well as an alchemical reaction triggered within the practitioner.

We will explore this kind of magic and its effects in much depth and practice in the final volume of the Holy Daimon cycle, *Holy Heretics* (Scarlet Imprint, 2021). In the current manuscript we find this notion of a lasting inner change expressed in the final paragraph of the first prayer:

> *Send me then the wisdom from your holy heavens, and from the throne of your sovereignty, that it may always be with me, working with me, that I may know what is pleasing to you. Amen.* (p. 2)

Condensed into the lines of what might seem to be a short opening prayer we indeed discover a whole magical program. Every word matters in texts like these; and often brevity and succinctness of thoughts are a direct expression of how much careful consideration and magical experience has shaped them.

Following this prayer, the father begins to introduce the reader/son to the general instructions. First, he explains that the lessons contained in this parcel allow for self-initiation into a *society of those who seek wisdom*. This society has a motto (truth and mercy), a number (75), a word (Vaudahat) and a nomination (Tiphareth), and each one expresses the quality of the Sephira of Tiphareth on the cabalistic Tree of Life (*Etz Chiim*).

Thus, we can conclude, this group of men works under the tutelage of the order of the angels called Malachim and stands in the classical position of the mediating priest: This is in between the triad of Divinity above and the triad of Creation below it, simultaneously enabling the balanced flow of tides of creation and destruction, as well as the structural balance of both sides of the generative forces of the Tree of Life. Both word and nomination are taken from Agrippa's *De Occulta Philosophia*[31]:

> *The sixt name is Eloha, or a name of four letters, joyned with Vaudahat, his numeration is Tiphereth, that is apparel, beauty, glory, pleasure, and signifieth the tree of life, and hath his influence through the order of vertues, which the Hebrews call Malachim, that is Angels into the spere of the Sun, giving brightness and life to it, and from thence producing mettals; his particular intelligence is Raphael, who was the Ruler of Isaac and Toby the younger, and the Angel Peliel, ruler of Iacob.*

The word *Vaudahat* represents a deformed writing of the Hebrew *ve-Da'ath* and is meant to be read as the Divine name *YHVH Eloah ve-Da'ath*, which traditionally is translated as *Lord God of Knowledge* and which expresses the manifestation of the Divine in the sphere of *knowledge* (Da'ath) and *balance* (Tiphareth).

The number 75 could also be read in kabbalistic terms, e.g. as a reference to the gematric value of the Hebrew word *Cohen*[32], thus hinting at the role of these wise men as acting priests of the forces of Tiphareth in the mundane world. However, such a reading is not only likely to have exceeded the kabbalistic knowledge of most

---

31 see Book III, page 369 of the 1651 edition

32 Kaph, 20 – He, 5 – Nun, 50

Christian-cabalistic occult orders at the time, but more importantly it would miss deciphering a much more important reference hidden in this number.

As mentioned above, our text stems from the circle of the original OGR members, possibly written by Schleiß von Löwenfeld himself.

One of the core tenets of their teachings relates to the purification and synthesis of the four elements within man, as it was deemed to prepare the 'human vessel' to come into communion with angelic consciousness.

Thus, the operation, if conducted successfully, was expressed by the image of the flaming star, the figure of the pentagram, or a rose with five petals.[33]

It is this very idea that we find encrypted within the number 75. To decipher it, we have to immerse ourselves in the material that was taught as part of their fourth degree, the 4°=7° Philosophus grade:

> *Die natürlichen Körper müssen durch eine sichtbare Reaktion aller 4 Elemente in 3 d.i. in Salz, Schwefel und Quecksilber, diese drei durch vier, d.i. durch die wirksamen Eigenschaften zur 7-Zahl, d.i. zur höchsten Klarheit in der Natur des reinsten Lichtwesens gebracht werden; damit sie durch die fortschreitende Wirkung der nunmehr gereinigten vier Elemente unzertrennlich wieder vereinigt und in die Natur der 5. Zahl, d.i. jener tincturalischen Quintessenz, wieder versetzt werden mögen, mit welcher selbe durch das schöpfende Wort ursprünglich begabt waren.*[34]

•

> *The natural bodies have to be transformed through a visible reaction of all 4 elements in 3, i.e. in salt, sulfur, and mercury, [and] these three through four, i.e. through the effective properties of the 7-number, which means they have to brought to the highest clarity in the nature of the purest light-being [Lichtwesen]; so that through the continuous*

---
33 Marx, 1930 p. 82/83

34 Nettelbladt, 1879, p. 528

> *impact of the purified four elements, they are inseparably reunited and incorporated again into the nature of the 5th number, i.e. that tinctural quintessence [tincturalischen Quintessenz], with which the latter originally had been endowed by the creative word.*[35]

What we find here is a complex amalgamation of astral, elemental and alchemical thinking, derived from sources that were paramount to the teachings of the OGR: Specifically Heinrich Cornelius Agrippa, Paracelsus, Jakob Böhme and Johannes Reuchlin.[36]

In essence the paragraph stipulates that the qualities of the four elements have to be purified through the skilful alchemical application of the three essential forces. Such successful process of purification and unification then is symbolised by the number 7, the coming together of the 4 and 3. However, this work remains in vitro if it only happens in the athanor of the alchemical art; if it is to have true efficacy and impact it needs to come to life in the inner nature of the adept himself.

Thus, we read that the 7 has to be reinstated within the 5, the pentagram and essential symbol of man. It is only this step that enables man to regain the empowerment that once was with him/her before the fall: The direct expression of the Divine creative word.

Now as often in magic, with a little effort it is viable to understand the broad outlines of most operations, but the devil is in the details. Men in particular have always loved the abstract purity of numerical allusions; but becoming real about what this means in everyday life is a whole different business. Just take the following differences in our key sources on how to actually interpret the forces expressed by the number 3, or the *Ternar.*

- Agrippa in his Book II, chapter 10 follows al-Kindi's interpretation and explains "the number three respects the soul, by reason of its threefold power, viz. rationale, irascible, and concupiscible." Thus, according to him numerologically 3

---

35 Nettelbladt, 1879, p. 528, translation by author

36 Marx, 1930, pp. 79

represents the essential forces endowed to the human soul: Intellect, anger and desire.

- Obviously we could also follow a different reading and adhere to Paracelsus's foundational tenet of the three essential building blocks of all material matter in creation, expressed as salt, sulphur, mercury. Purifying the four elements of their adhesion to these substance-generating principles is a highly complex operation, requiring a thorough understanding of Paracelsus's unique cosmology. We will delve deeper into it in the final part of the Holy Daimon Cycle, *Holy Heretics* (Scarlet Imprint, 2021).

- And just to make things even more complicated: Alternatively we could also reference Jakob Böhme who dedicated more than 500 pages to describing the three divine principles emanating all of creation and beyond (*Drei Prinzipien*, 1619). Böhme still knows and elaborates on the three Paracelsian principles (salt, mercury, sulfur). However, he also evolves the concept further and introduces us to another kind of Ternar: With Böhme we encounter the two opposing forces of Solve et Coagula as well as a third force, which he describes as a bitter quality of fear which generates all matter and actually encompasses all three Paracelsian principles.[37]

Luckily our author avoids much of these speculations, and delves right into what walking the path of Tiphareth requires in practice: First, that it is a path which is walked outside any formal, man-made constructs. Or as the text says, *no constitutions or written rules, no convents or lodges* guide the walker. No superiors, no secretary, no seal, no oath exist. No one is neither initiated nor excommunicated by anyone else; and no ceremonies unite its members. Furthermore, the author switches tenses, from past into present and back; thus leaving further ambiguity over whether he presents a report of a society that once existed or one that continues to be active.

---

37 Marx, 1930, p. 95

> *We do not accept anyone, everyone accepts himself according to the degree of love he gives himself through his actions, according to this he transfers himself into the higher or lower degree of Divine Approximation.* […]
>
> *We exclude no one; everyone excludes himself by the degree of distance to which he descends again when he leaves truth and mercy.* (p. 3)

The introduction is unmistakably clear as to why the father/author had stressed that the son/reader needed to be a mature adult when opening this occult parcel. What we encounter here is not an introduction to the vestibule of the temple, but *to the highest level of the temple* (p. 3). Walking a path that is not outlined by any man-made markers of orientation, but only guided by our own ability to bring through the Divine qualities of the sephira of Tiphareth is indeed the work of the adept.

The texts warns against outer or formal occult societies, the ones relating to the Masonic tradition in particular, and explains how their original intentions and claims had quickly become corrupted. Equally, the necessity to cloak occult mysteries in cryptic symbols and intricate emblems ceases to exist if the walker can behold the Divine Light directly. The required qualities of the adept on this journey are fourfold: (1, FIRE) a strong will and determination, (2, AIR) technical mastery of entering a state of gnosis, (3, WATER) a ceaseless desire for Divine wisdom, greater than the attachment to one's own ego and, finally, (4, EARTH) the ability to continuously express active love in one's words and deeds, even if faced with adversity and lack of reciprocity from one's fellow humans.

> *If these qualities are united within head, heart and hand of the practitioner, the author explains, "wisdom will receive you into her bosom." And they will begin to learn "to germinate the highest levels of man's happiness — this happiness is the true in knowledge and the good in practice — and simultaneously [you will] enjoy the benefits that the true and good grant to you.* (p. 3)

At this moment the aspiring adept becomes a companion to all adepts who travelled on this path before them. They become a living link in the eternal chain. Again, the text uses its language incredibly carefully and is deliberately ambiguous in this section: We do not know if the German term for *company* (*Gesellschaft*) is meant to indicate the above mentioned invisible society in the present day, or whether it refers to a spiritual companionship beyond the borders of time and space.

> [...] *an angel whom Wisdom sends to lead you will be your guide; never make yourself unworthy of his presence. You will recall that we have neither ceremonies nor temple, – our temple is the world, our ceremonies are the practice of the works of love.*
>
> [...]
>
> •
>
> *Our bond is the bond of love that unites man with man, and man with angels and God. My son! Alike is chained to alike – similar to similar – you shall be connected with your alike, with your similar, according to the degree of your love.* (p. 4)

It is the last section here that cannot be overemphasised in terms of its practical relevance and magical impact. Practitioners who have come to understand these two sentences through first-hand experience (rather than abstract cognitive considerations alone) will be able to elevate their work to superior levels of simplicity and impact.

More than anything, the practical knowledge of this sentence is what distinguishes the adept from the initiate: To derive everyday practice and virtuous habits from the essential insight that alike attracts alike, and thus, that the quality of our own presence determines the quality of spirits we are naturally enabled to commune with.

> *The more your spirituality opens you up, the more you will receive supernatural knowledge; you will be guided by exalted beings* [in harmony with your own state of spiritual presence]. (p. 4)

To expand further on this idea, we quote a section from a source-work that had critical impact on the teachings of the Order of the Golden and Rosy Cross, Georg von Welling's *Opus mago-cabbalisticum et theologicum* (1735).

> *Conversation with such spirits is not as easily done today, as many foolish conjurers and sorcerers might imagine: But putting all such devilry aside, you should know that anyone who would dare to undertake such things must have, in addition to a true inner fear of God, also complete gnosis [Erkenntnis] of the truthful Magical Service. He must be deeply experienced in the true philosophia, so that he knows absolutely the true and most reduced essence of each element, so that he knows what is pleasing and repelling to each kind of these spirit-humans in their elements, in order to suppress the repelling and exalt the pleasing, as we experience and behold daily even with the wild animals, each of them can be excited, attracted and finally trapped through the use of a particular scent; yet something repugnant to them would only drive them away. He has to be a cabalistic mage [Magus Cabalist] and true theosopher to be entirely familiar with the characteristics of the spirits [Characteristicatio Spirituum], for the devil not to fool them; and once he has these characteristics, he will also be a true astrologer, as this is essentially required in this secret art, he has to become familiar with a sacred reclusion, and know how to sharpen their imagination to the most exalted degree, so he quasi might encounter these spirit-humans by his imaginative vibrancy [Radios Imaginationis suae] and through it, almost as if it were a strong magnet, attract these to himself; for true faith is nothing other than the pure vibrancy of our imagination when entirely immersed into the Divine Light. For whatever our imagination is directed towards sharply, therein it takes effect; and this secret is the ground and the base of the sacred art of magic and cabbala within the secret theology.*[38]

Our general discussion concludes with a more detailed explanation of the *last and supreme symbol*; a seal the son/ reader is meant to

---

38 Georg von Welling, *Opus mago-cabbalisticum et theologicum*, 1735, translation by author

have cast in gold and wear on a ribbon on their side as a constant reminder of their duties as both a human and an adept. Equally, they are invited to have the symbol worked into a seal for use in written correspondence, so brothers in spirit could recognise each other more easily. The original version of this symbol has been lost; we only have copied drawings from Beyer's publication in 1930, executed by a fellow Freemason, Carl Kämpe. For this essay, we have commissioned a new version of the seal, authentic to the original instructions, yet executed by the inspired and masterful hand of *Jose Gabriel Alegría Sabogal*. The slight adjustments we deliberately introduced were to change the term on the petal on the right/East from *[love your] prince and fatherland* to *[love] what governs you*; as well as to adjust the overall language from German or French respectively to Classical Latin.

On a path which is walked entirely by oneself, empty-handed, and only judged by Divinity, we hope this *supreme symbol* will continue to be used in its authentic sense: As a constant reminder to ourselves about our duties as humans and adepts; and just as much as a symbol of identification for brothers and sisters on the same journey.

> *So take this sign, my son, from your father's hand, and bind it to your side with a band of fire-coloured ribbon, and wear it as a constant reminder of your duties.*
>
> *The colour of the ribbon reminds you that your zeal shall never cool down, like the fire of your love.*
>
> *Purify your heart, gather your soul, choose solitude, and pray to God – and make yourself worthy to receive the highest degree of the holy magic.* (p. 5)

The closing of the General Instructions encourage the son/reader to destroy the papers after reading them. Another reminder that the path ahead was not about study in books written by men, but the book of (one's celestial) nature. Thus, active guidance from here onwards should not be expected to come from paper and ink, but from the *angel of light* at one's side.

Similarily, the famous advice Johannes Trithemius gave to Agrippa of Nettesheim, upon the latter's planned publication of his *De Occulta Philosophia* is echoed: To remain silent about one's path and the secrets endowed upon oneself. Because *the crumbs that fall from the table of the Godhead are not for the pigs that rummage in the dung;* and through a more humanist perspective the father/author adds in the voice of the Apostle Paul, *not everything that is good is also good for everyone* (p. 6).

> *"Everything is permissible," but not everything is beneficial. "Everything is permissible," but not everything is edifying. No one should seek his own good, but the good of others.*[39]

3. Initiation

The present ritual of self-initiation is written for the advanced initiate, wishing to become an adept on the path of the empty hand. We need not dissect the ritual in all its components nor provide a detailed walk-through, as sufficient detail for the experienced practitioner is provided by the text itself. Instead, we will focus on the historic context in which such self-initiation rituals may be read to reveal a deeper understanding.

Echoes of Ancient Jewish Magic

The opening of the ritual consists of a threefold sequence of undressing, performing a sevenfold ablution or purification, and putting on the ritual garment symbolic of the *new man*.

Using the symbol and image of ritual garments to support an initiatory transformation of identity can be traced back far in time. One of the most striking examples we can find is the Jewish *Sefer ha-Malbush* (*Book of the Garment*) which circulated among the Medieval Hasidim of Ashkenaz. Already Gershom Sholem characterised

---

39 Corinthians 10:23/24

their occult tradition in the 12th and 13th century as highly syncretic in nature:

> *All sorts of traditions, difficult to trace in their origins and of occult cultural imprint, swam along here, and in the strangest way here ancient Jewish magic is becoming integrated with Hellenistic occultism and the entirety of Old German magic and demon beliefs, which one often encounters in contemporary literature.*[40]

Now in the Sefer ha-Malbush, after a first seven-day period of abstinence, the adept is instructed to create a ritual garment, connected to a turban, both made of gazelle-parchment. This vestment is to be inscribed in a circular fashion with the *great and terrible name*. What follows, both for the inscription of the garment and the attached turban, are lengthy combinations of Jewish divine names, permutations of the Tetragrammaton as well as *nomina barbara*.[41]

After a second period of abstinence and seclusion, on the night of the eighth day the initiate is guided to walk to an open water and meditate in silence. If a particular spirit reveals itself in the air right above the water surface, then they are encouraged to walk into the water up to their hips, there to don the ritual garment. Standing in the water at night, dressed in the divine names, the initiate is then instructed to conjure the names of ten angels.

Initially, the initiate will see nothing but smoke. However, once the angels are fully present, the initiate can ask them to appear in a particular form. During that night the angels will commune with the initiate for a maximum of three to four hours. Faithfully observing the rules of purity given at the beginning will enable the adept to command these angels for seven more days to come.[42]

Despite the differences in historic time and cultural milieu we find several notable links between our text and the Sefer ha-Malbush: Most importantly, these are (a) the central practice of using a ritual

40 Scholem, 2000, p. 93
41 Wandrey, 2004, p. 147/165
42 Wandrey, 2004, p. 147-150

garment to *put on* a new spiritual identity and to facilitate interspecies communion, (b) the importance of ritual purity, the role of water and a sevenfold structure to the preparatory stage[43], (c) the conjuration of ten kabbalistic angelic ranks to assist the practitioner in the operation, and finally (d) the simple fact that both rituals are of explicitly self-initiatory nature, requiring no social facilitation or other kind of human agency.

It is not our intention to insinuate our current author, writing from within the context of the Order of the Golden and Rosy Cross, deliberately leveraged the Sefer ha-Malbush as a ritualistic precursor. The use of ritual garments as magical objects obviously can be traced back much further in time[44]; just as much as it can be found much closer to the origin of our text as we shall see later on.

What we do want to point out though is the axiom that magical practices which work, i.e. which achieve the intended results, often know few boundaries in terms of time, culture or religion. Parallels in practice do not always speak to written lineage or even verbal tradition; yet often they illustrate the consistent ontological dynamics underlying all magical practice.

> *'Putting on the name' has to be understood here in a dual sense: On the one hand, it means to put on the garment onto which the esoteric names of God have been written, but on the other hand it also means to use the power inherent in God. The name of God and His being belong together.*[45]

After the ritualist has been undressed of the *old man*, cleansed seven times, purified with the "dew of heaven" and are robed in the "garment of innocence", the main section of the ritual commences.

This consist of ten prayers directed to the Sephiroth on the kabbalistic Tree of Life. The sequence follows the lightning flash from

---

43 Wandrey, 2004, p. 153

44 e.g. PGM I/279, PGM IV/930 or even Apuleius's *Metamorphosis*, Book XI, Chapter XIV

45 Wandrey, 2004, p. 176

Kether to Malkuth, touching upon each sephirah upon its path into manifestation. As expected in classical Kabbala, the 11th pseudo-sephirah of Da'ath is omitted. The actual text that makes up the respective prayers is mainly quoted from Agrippa's *De Occulta Philosophia* where it appears in *Book Three, Chapter X*.

However, where in Agrippa's work we find a simple list and concise description of all sephiroth, their divine names, angelic rulers, etc, our text elevates these descriptions and turns them into direct addresses towards the mentioned entities. Thus, for each of the ten sephiroth the practitioner calls out to the specific divine manifestation, their angelic orders, archangels, etc.

By the end of the ten invocations the ritualist has not only immersed themselves into the presence of about thirty different spiritual entities, but conjured up the presence of the entire cosmos as manifested by the governing forces of each sephirah.

In addition to the introductory process of wearing the *garment of innocence*, it is also the sequence of these ten prayers which seals access to the forces behind this ritual for any unexperienced practitioner: Just reading out the prayers obviously will do very little; the aspiring adept, in a state of gnosis, is meant to direct their gaze towards the Divine Light and utter or sing these hymnal prayers into the light.

Like many initiations, such kind of ritual looks deceptively simple on the outside, yet demands a lot from the practitioner, and is meant to be performed only once in a lifetime.

> *With the burning of each incense take the seal and table of the spirit in your hand, and ask God for the respective degree of sanctification.*
> (p. 7)

As assistance in this process, the text mentions that the practitioner can leverage an unidentified set of seals as well as a *table of the spirit*. Unfortunately, these two tools have either been lost or were never part of the original text. They would have acted respectively as visual focus point and textual memory aid for the practitioner in the lengthy process of reciting all ten prayers. Be that as it may, their loss still leaves the ritual perfectly intact for operation.

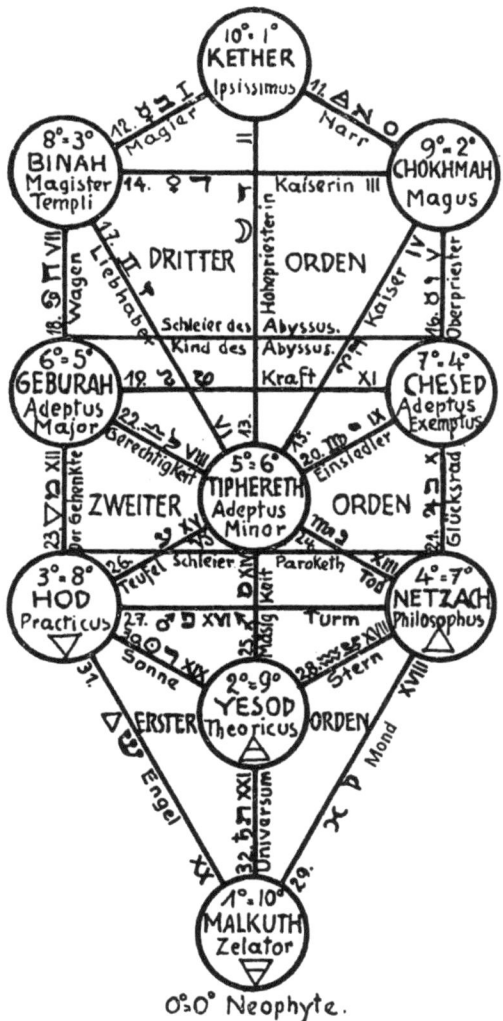

The Tree of Life and the grade structure of the Order of the Golden and Rosy Cross, source: Marx, Arnold; *Die Gold- und Rosenkreuzer – Ein Mysterienbund des ausgehenden 18. Jahrhunderts*, in: Bernhard Beyer, *Das Freimaurer-Museum, Band V*, 1930, p. 62

The integrity of the ritual text, in absence of magical seals or summarising tables, becomes evident when we compare it to a second reference point of Medieval Jewish Mysticism: This is Joseph ben Abraham Gikatilla's (1248 – after 1305) seminal work *Gates of Light* (*Sha'are orah*).

First translated into Latin in 1587 by Johannes Pistorius, the *Porta Lucis* quickly became a cornerstone of Christian Kabbala. In stark contrast to the cryptic and often allegorical style of the *Zohar*, Gikatilla dared to provide a highly accessible account of Jewish Mysticism at his time, as well as a detailed exploration of the realms of the ten sephiroth, i.e. the gates of light in particular.

Thus, his most prominent work, while written in the contemporary style of medieval philosophical works in the 13th century, presented an entire *encyclopaedia of God Names*, a map into the mystical pathways in the form of a *systemic, clear, detailed work* which allowed access to kabbalistic teachings far beyond *only the elect few*.[46]

> *Joseph the son of Abraham Gikatilla opens his work Gates of Light by gently chastising a disciple who wishes to know Kabbalistic wisdom but for the wrong reasons. The study of Kabbalah, which requires knowing and meditating on the different attributes and Names of God, was not to be used to manipulate the natural world for personal gain, as Gikatilla's disciple had wanted. Rather, one sought Kabbalistic wisdom in order to become intimate with the Holy One, for only through knowing Him intimately might one be blessed.*[47]

Again we encounter formal similarities to the current text, which could be accidental or deliberately intended by our author: Just like our testament so Gikatilla's work is addressed to a younger student, and just like our manuscript so the author of the Gates of Light warns his reader against the risk of leveraging mystical powers to engage in natural magic, but urging the reader instad to stay on the direct path towards personal communion with Divinity.

---

46 Avi Weinstein, in: Gikatilla, 1994, xvii
47 Avi Weinstein, in: Gikatilla, 1994, xvii

Most obvious is the similarity in terms of textual structure: Just like our text so Gikatilla allows the reader to pass through the ten gates of the sephiroth, with the marked difference that the latter is approaching the Tree of Life from its base in Malkuth, while our text begins with Kether at the top of its crown.

> *'Gates of Light' presents the novice with a strategy for intimacy with his Creator.*[48]

The most important aspect though is that in Gikatilla's work we encounter the same double function embedded in our present work: His detailed reflections upon the ten gates of light indeed provide invaluable information to the aspiring as well as the advanced student of Kabbala; at the same time they provide an outline of gnostic meditations intended for the mystical practitioner. The value of the book lies both in its encyclopaedic depth of information, and in the mystical map it provides for practical explorations. Divine wisdom can not only be gained through the Gates of Light by detailed study, it can also be accessed by practice. Gikatilla himself gives us this hint in his opening remarks to the daring student; noting that this book not only contains keys to unlocking knowledge of the head, but also to wisdom of the heart.

> *When you have learned this, then God will answer when you call. You will be one of those who are truly close to Him and you will love Him with all your heart. Yes, you will delight in YHVH, and He will grant you all that you ask.*[49]

It is precisely in this spirit that our author, more than five hundred years after Gikatilla, takes what seemed to be a plain table of divine names and angelic ranks in Agrippa's second book, and turns it into a sequence of kabbalistic hymns meant to be sung out to the very spirits they describe.

Obviously, Gikatilla knew well enough not to include artificial seals or simplistic tables in his work; for both are tools that invite

---

48 Avi Weinstein, in: Gikatilla, 1994, xx

49 Gikatilla, 1994, p. 3

skimming over the text and visual distraction much more than spelling the text out with the lips of one's heart.

> *So, after we have given over the keys contained in this introduction to you, we must now go forth and explain each of the Holy Names as they are written in the Torah. We must enlighten your eyes concerning every place where they may be found, so that you will understand and be aware of the well of living waters which flows from all His blessed Names. And when you grasp this message then you will succeed in your ways and you will be enlightened.* [50]

Echoes of Rosicrucian Magic

> *Now how does one acquire the magical power, by means of which one can force spirits into service, and when many magicians work together, transplant the Kingdom of God to the earth, make gods of men and a paradise of the world? – The magical power is sometimes declared to be innate, sometimes transferable, sometimes a gift of grace from above, sometimes the result of a mysterious teaching or moral and ritual exercises. Petty and outer magicians have used and advised petty means; deep spirits have recognised that the magical power is based on the unification of the I with the Thou, on the alignment of our will with the divine will, as the mystic Jeane Leade expressed it. Such a will can effect everything, can bind and release, heal and spoil, nothing resists it. Jakob Böhme and before him Paracelsus called the magical power "imagination" [...]. With the help of the imagination, Paracelsus believed that man could pull down the stars, conjure spirits and exert any other effect. In principle, Pico and Reuchlin, Agrippa and Fludd, Bruna and Comenius thought no differently, to disregard the ancient philosophers and theurgists.*

> *All of them, and with them the magicians of lesser rank, were convinced of God's help and approval in the acts of white magic and*

---

50 Gikatilla, 1994, p. 9

considered themselves good Christians. Prayer and immersion in God were considered to be the main means of acquiring and strengthening magical power. The Christian God and his flocks were their allies; in their name the spirits were conjured, even the incantations were arranged as proper divine services. One could wonderfully prove and justify the doctrine of the intermediate beings from the Bible. In the Bible one read about dynasties of angels and devils, and it was not difficult, with the help of gnostic and kabbalistic speculations, to expand these allusions to a huge, cascaded system of spirits (intelligences, emanations) that filled the gap between the highest God and the short-lived people dependent on the senses. To enter into communication with the spirit realm, to rise up to it and to win the powers of ever more powerful spirits for oneself, seemed to be an endeavour quite worthy of the Christian and friend of God.[51]

These are the general explanations on Late Medieval *white magic* by the philosopher and mystic August Horneffer (1875-1955) in his book *Symbolism of the Mystery Cults*.[52]

Now, whether such a thing as authentic *Rosicrucian Magic* actually exists is of course just as debatable as the origin of this mythical group of adepts in the late 16th and early 17th century. Most likely, it would have to be acknowledged as a retrospective historic construct that converged and amalgamated the writings and influences of liminal figures such as Johannes Tauler, Johannes Trithemius, Paracelsus, Jacob Böhme and other German mystics of the first century of the Protestant Reformation.

Despite the colourful and diverse seeds that blossomed into the loose bouquet of the Early Modern Rosicrucian current, we can clearly identify several unique characteristics which distinguished it from other parallel currents of mago-mystical practice of the time - and actually continue to do so even in the modern day.

---

51 Horneffer, 1924, p. 218/219, translation by Frater Acher
52 *Symbolik der Geheimbünde*, Heidelberg: Niels Kampmann Verlag, 1924

From a historic perspective, the most obvious point might be that we can position Rosicrucian as a counter-current to the emerging *grimoire magic* from the late 16th to 18th century: Epitomised by the ambiguous figure of Johann Georg Faust (1466 – c. 1541), the following centuries built upon his sinister fame and originated an entire genre of magical (pseudo-)grimoires, which to this day enjoys commercial success despite its often featherweight content.

In stark contrast to these, magic performed in the spirit of the Rosicrucian current built upon the original magical program of Johannes Trithemius, to establish a practice of white magic within a reformed spirit of Christianity.[53]

With that purpose in mind, it would produce genuinely new artefacts such as the famous *Arbatel* (1575), as well as incorporate strong influences of Paracelsus's take on alchemy, astrology and natural magic, Christian Kabbala and obviously Hermeticism. While the term Rosicrucian magic never came to signify of a genre of its own, it does help distinguish it from the specifically magical practices of a wider current known as original Theosophy. We have quoted above from one of its later main sources, Georg von Welling's *Opus Mago-Cabbalisticum et Theosophicum* (1735).

Carlos Gilly in his introduction to Heinrich Khunrath's *Amphitheatrum Sapientiae Aeternae* (1595) gives us a succinct summary of this broader spiritual current:

> *From the middle of the 16th until the 18th century Theosophy represents the attempt to walk the worldly way of gnosis (Gotteserkenntnis) which has been neglected by theology: the way of exploring nature in order to achieve gnosis of God. At the same time Theosophy refers to the application of these insights in order to achieve a more intimate vision of reality and thus to generate new knowledge about nature. The recoining of this term by more modern movements in the 19th and 20th century should not make us forget that since the publication of Balthasar Flötter's edition of the philosophia magna by*

---

53 see Acher, 2020

> *Paracelsus 1567, the publication of the book Arbatel in 1575 and since the emergence of Johann Arndt's De antique philosophia ca. 1580 'Theosophy' (and not 'Pansophy', 'Cosmosophy' and similar more recent expressions) had been a highly precise term referring to a movement extending from Paracelsus to Weigl, Arndt, Sclei, Crollius, Haslmayr, Nollius, Hirsch, Fludd, Böhme, Franckenberg, van Helmont, Kozák, Comenius all the way to Maul, Welling and Oetinger - while not forgetting the 'Brotherhood of Theosophists of the RosyCross' (Brüderschaft der Theosophen vom RosenCreutz) as mentioned by Adam Haslmayr.*[54]

And one more time, let's also hear Horneffer's early 20th century summary of the kind of magical reformation to which he believed the early Rosicrucians aspired:

> *Magic was also practiced by the Rosicrucians; however, the mysterious Rosicrucian movement was probably actually directed towards something else. The magician's work consisted in establishing direct contact with the spirit world, over which he gained power and which he aimed to join as a superhuman or god-man. The Rosicrucian's work consisted in the transformation and refinement of nature, as a result of which he hoped for a "general reformation of the whole world". [...]*
>
> *Since the 16th century, alchemy was also called the "spagyric art", i.e. the art of separating and joining together. Since the world, as man finds it, is already cosmically ordered and each thing has its rightful place in the whole, order is disturbed and dissolved by the work: The holy worker separates what belongs together, he dissolves the world into its elements, he kills living things and makes chaos out of the cosmos by his intervention. So the boat builder who cuts down trees, so the alchemist who melts down metals or extracts the prima materia from a natural object, so the bricklayer who crushes the rock in the mountain to make stones. Out of chaos he then creates a new order and beauty; he reassembles the separated and destroyed into a higher, more planned, divine unity. Thus the cathedral is a cosmos higher*

---

54 Gilly, 2014, p. 11, translation by author

> *than the quarry, the barge higher than the tree, the philosopher's stone higher than any other natural or artificial object used in its preparation.*[55]

We have placed Horneffer's elucidations here to illustrate how hard it is today to regain access to the original spirit of what we believe should be called Rosicrucian Magic. For in Horneffer's interpretation man has not turned into a modest spirit-worker, but into a *superman* unleashed: Rather than humbly stepping into the chain of creation, according to Horneffer, the adept holds divine empowerment to destroy and rebuild the world entirely.

Obviously, such interpretation could not stand further apart from what we read in e.g. Paracelsus's approach to the philosophia adepti. Unsurprisingly therefore, in the roughly hundred years since Horneffer published his at the time very 'en vogue' interpretation of the Great Work, we have collected ample evidence for the devastating and not at all transformative or refining impact of such an approach to the work. From two world wars, via the destructive impact of global industrial and ecological exploitation, to the far-reaching negative side effects of approaching agriculture as if we were divine spagyric alchemists, it has become obvious that a misinterpretation of the Rosicrucian work leads not to man standing before the throne of Divinity, but to man placing himself upon it.

With such pitfalls and modern misinterpretations in mind, let's attempt to restore a more original, a more authentic version of what Tauler, Trithemius, Paracelsus, etc. understood to be proper spirit work, and as we will see, this will lead us right back to our manuscript at hand, and possibly allow us to reread it with an altogether different view.

So let's get to the heart of the matter: The defining feature of Rosicrucian Magic, as we have used the term in our manifest of the same name (Chapter 6), is that it breaks the age-old supposed opposition of mystical practices leading away from the world (evolu-

---

55 Horneffer, 1924, p. 226/227, translation by author

tion), and magical ones creating greater proximity to it (involution). Rather Rosicrucian Magic aspired to integrate both aspects: *To balance the fulcrum of being fully involved in the physical, as well as deeply present in the spiritual realm.*

Thus, Rosicrucian Magic did not become an elite escape route from the seeming chaos and pain of the physical realm, and neither did it attempt, in the spirit of August Horneffer or Julius Evola, to restore control over these volatile forces; even in the small circumference of the practitioner's own life. Instead, it tore down the wall between everyday life and the magical circle, and came to understand every act as equally mundane and magical, secular and sacred.

Similar to the everyday experience of members of indigenous animistic tribes, the practitioner of Rosicrucian Magic did not need to do anything special to constantly be surrounded by spirits and to communicate with them: Each interaction with the world was an interaction with the spirit of nature in its myriad forms of existence.

Applying oneself with grace and beauty, with calm and purpose, with deep humility and in divine service to the world was the way of the adept. Not for their own sake; the adepts do this, not to secure a place in heaven in the afterlife, or to create a stage of particular purity for the next magical rite, but because the ripples our actions send into the world, cause the world to respond back to everyone.

The problem with this concept is that it was misunderstood as a metaphor early on. The light of nature turned into the book of nature and then the book became a science. The foundations of Rosicrucian Magic, however, rest on the premise of the experience of the world as dialogue. Whatever the primal ontological essence of nature might be, as human beings, if we decide to speak to each natural object around us as a being in its own right, they will respond back to us in that very same way. And yet their answers and influences will be most surprising! Very rarely will we find affirmation of our own beliefs, and much more often the same tension, difficulty and dynamics as we encounter in human-to-human dialogue.

Encountering nature through the lens of Rosicrucian Magic is not a flight of fancy, it is precisely not the threshold that leads us into happy-land, filled with human superpowers. Rather it opens access to a different realm, a lower or higher (depending on one's journey and reference frames) version of the same reality we are already caught up in. Only that in this version of the world everything is gifted with intelligence, with the ability to speak, listen and respond. We level the playing field of all the temporal borders erected by differences in times, blood, species, genre, types, etc. Everyone can speak to anyone here. While certainly not safe from misunderstandings, disaccords and dread, we at least lift the veil of blindness, and stop being isolated from the world through our state of being human, rather than becoming a spirit like everything else.

With all the above in mind, it might be useful to read Schleiß von Löwenfeld's ritual instructions to his son a second time. Please feel invited to pause right here, to return to the previous chapter and to read the full ritual instructions one more time.

While taking each sentence in, consider each step described as a conscious act of Rosicrucian Magic: The undressing of our humanness, the stepping into our role as servants, aspiring to stand before the throne of Divinity, the becoming part of "the society of those who seek wisdom" and the embrace of the number 75 and the word Vaudahat. Then the act of courage, the dangers of stepping forward – and calling out to the ten spheres of divine creation directly, with its dozens of beings, all being called into presence around us. Now we see the adept standing surrounded by all facets of life. And each facet is a hive being with millions of eyes looking at them. Dare we stand that exposed, that naked, face to face with the primal world as it has always been?

If every mundane act is already an act of magic, performing a deeply contacted ritual like the one at hand becomes the event of a life-time. There is no returning from it, and nobody holds responsibility for approaching these raw forces of nature in such a naked state, but us. Better not to do it, if we cannot see the magic yet of touching a flower, of speaking to the wind or listening to a river. This ritual is a needle full of ink, ready to be placed on the skin of our soul. We better have trained the hand that holds it, as well as the soul that will carry its sign. After all, the best thing in magic is that we have countless lives to learn, to understand and to perfect it. Never in magic is there a reason to rush. Ever.

Clearly this world does not need more tearing down, more destruction, only to suffer the flawed attempts of being rebuilt according to human hubris. Instead, we'd like to propose, this world needs us to listen, and if we dare and can bear the consequences, to invite the choir of all its ten realms into the fragile sphere of our heart-flame.

May we all travel well.

The Closing

The significance of the event activated with this ritual is symbolically emphasised again at its very end. Here we are asked to wash a ring with dew and the smoke of incense, before proclaiming it the symbol of the "bond of union between me and the Holy Angels of the Godhead". For just like in the spiritual ideal of a marriage we have made our soul bond with others, and placed ourselves under a tutelage which is now irreversible.

The ties between us and the angelic realm of creation are further symbolised by the three coloured ribbons which we are asked to braid into one; and place our prayer upon it:

> *My God! Grant me your grace that I may unite my physical, visible and spiritual life according to your holy intentions and become worthy of the great grace of sanctification.*
>
> *Then burn this ribbon and say: As no human hand has broken this covenant, so no earthly power can break my covenant with God and the Angels.*

After literally having burned all the bridges to our old selves and lives, we take two final ribbons, one black, one white. The black one we tear apart as a symbol of the chain that had held us tied to darkness, and no longer has the power to do so. After burning it, we tie the white one around our forehead and speak:

My God! Purify my soul and bind me with the bond of innocence with your Holy Angels.

As these symbolic acts are performed directly following the main invocation of the ten divine spheres, they will be heavily charged with magic. The practitioner will still experience them not only as a most extraordinary moment, but as the physical seal over a most radical spiritual decision.

We invite meditation over the inner experiences each ribbon represents; and how one could perform the adequate action in vision while following the physical instructions above? After all, the spirits surrounding us in this very moment will first see the hands of our soul, before they see our organic body. Ensuring all aspects of our being are tied into these acts is the mystery of magical trance, and can only be learned and mastered by each one of us alone.

Then light the altar of sacrifice and say: Everything is vain except loving and serving God alone.

Then destroy the altar, and say: From now on my heart shall be the temple of God, and my altar [shall be] my love. Amen.

Finally, having arrived at the end of this initiation, we destroy the altar of our operation. As we remarked above, operations like this one will only be worked once in our life-times. Furthermore, following this ritual, it is unlikely the operator will have any good use for a magical altar over many months and years to come. We have turned ourselves into a fresh seedling. What we now need is not more magic, but time to learn how to see the world through the new eyes we have been granted.

•

Q. Where are you from?

Answ. From Bensalem.

Q. Where is the place?

Answ. In the orient, apart from the people.

Q. Why in the orient [East]?

Answ. Because the light comes from the beginning.

Q. Is it daytime in Bensalem?

Answ. The sun is at high-noon.

Q. Is it night in Bensalem?

Answ. No – because the sun always shines in the centre.

Q. Is there a temple in Bensalem?

Answ. There is no temple in the heart of man.

Q. What is the inscription?

Answ. Truth and Goodness.

Q. What was my business in Bensalem?

Answ. To cast off the old man and be born again.

Chapter 6.

Rosicrucian Magic. A Manifesto.

Let's begin with an exercise.

Think of an equal-armed cross, and yourself standing in its middle. You turn towards the North and begin to divest yourself of all aspects of your being that belong into this realm: Your past, your roots and ancestors, your bodily strength and integrity. All things float back over this threshold that shield and contain: Your skin, your bones, your blood. When there is nothing left to give to the North, whatever is left of you turns towards the East. Here you continue the process: You hand over your familiar thought patterns, your intellect and mind, your ability to speak and utter, until you no longer remember your own name.

Then, whatever is left of you turns towards the South and divest the aspects of yourself that belong here: Your future, that path leading ahead, your desires and fire, and all the chapters to come in your book of life.

Now the little of yourself that still stands in the centre turns towards the West. Immediately the cells of your being that came from here begin to float back over the threshold of their origin: Your emotional weave, your traumas and delights, your love and anger, and the invisible substance from which – countless times without realising – you have created, destroyed and rebuilt that fragile sense of meaning.

What is left of you now, what finally returns to the centre, is nothing but a dim light. One breath of wind and your spark would be gone. Naked, vulnerable, almost unborn again, your light hovers in the centre of the cross.

There a ripple returns from the four quarters, as well as from below and above. And the spark that is an echo of your essence lights up, and unfolds into the form of a rose-bud. No roots, no stalk, no leaves, just a flower waiting to be awoken, hovering in the middle of the cross.

That is the mystery of the Rosy-Cross: For standing in its centre means giving up a lot of ourselves. It means no longer having the luxury of being oriented by the quarters; by ones own hand or heart or head. The one who has become the rose knows no directions any longer, and above and below have fallen into one. All that remains is the dim light shining forth from ourselves, waiting to hear the echo of Divinity.

Speaking of *Rosicrucian Magic* is a folly for many good reasons. It's best to be avoided to be honest. Most people, scholars and practitioners alike, quickly came to substitute it with terms such as *Theosophy*, *Pansophy*, *Astronomia Olympi* more rarely, or simply *adepta philosophia*.

So if we dare using these two often romanticised and rarely understood terms here bound into one — Rosicrucian and Magic — it is for one reason alone. Because, if properly understood, nothing describes the essence of the work better than this simple term. The four arms of the cross span the world, they uphold its necessary tides and tensions; the rose is our work.

We would like this term to be understood as referring to the practical magical legacy left behind by great adepts such as Johannes Tauler, Johannes Trithemius, Paracelsus, Jacob Böhme and many other, now nameless German mystics of the first and second century of the Protestant Reformation. We are precisely not referring to any occult order, any organisation known by seal and stamp, nor even any magical lineage. We are referring to a light that came through with these humans, shining in their works and words, and which, if we let it, can guide us again today.

Rosicrucian Magic, as we like to apply the term, can be many things to many people, and yet, it is one thing above all: It is the

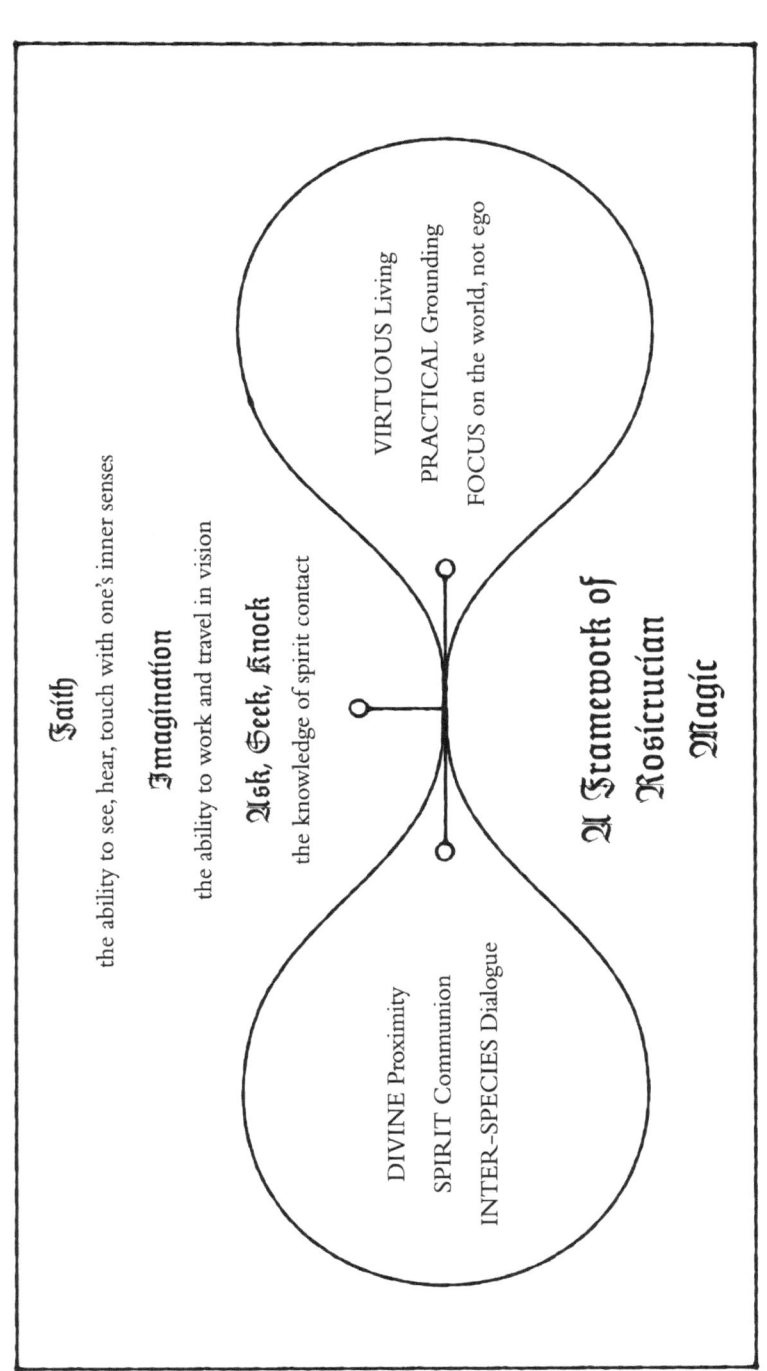

magical work that ripples out from the rose-bud described above, void of human motives, void of the ever hungry I, Me and Mine, void of roots and times past, void also of eyes seeing a path.

Rosicrucian Magic requires us to master three tools, which when used together from the centre of the cross, allow us to balance the fulcrum of being fully involved in the physical, as well as deeply present in the spiritual realm. It operates on the premise that everything is always present – or can be awakened – and that each thing created holds a spark of consciousness and presence of its own. Thus, everything wants to be spoken to, and everything wants to be heard. Silence and listening are at the heart of this craft; just as learning how to not apply its power.

If we wanted to condense it into a most simple framework, and this is the intent of this short text, it could look like the following: The choices we make on the right, the world we encounter on the left, the fulcrum of our craft at its centre. Left and right, bound into one by necessity, organically react to each other like the arms of a scale: You make a movement on the right, you see its countermovement on the left, and vice versa.

Spirit work is everyday work. The scent of your will attracts beings alike. The impression of your deed creates a hollow for the spirits to follow: One word uttered, a million ears pricked; one arrow shot, a hive of spirits awaiting its impact.

Rosicrucian Magic is born from the deep realisation that we cannot be part of this world, without forever changing it. None of us will ever walk over snow without leaving a trace. Rather, we have to come to terms with the fact that each of our acts is both mundane and magical, secular and sacred at once. Right at the same time, in every second, with every breath, we are being born from the outside just as much as from the inside.

If all of this sounds a little too abstract, let me invite you to meditate over the diagrams on the next page.

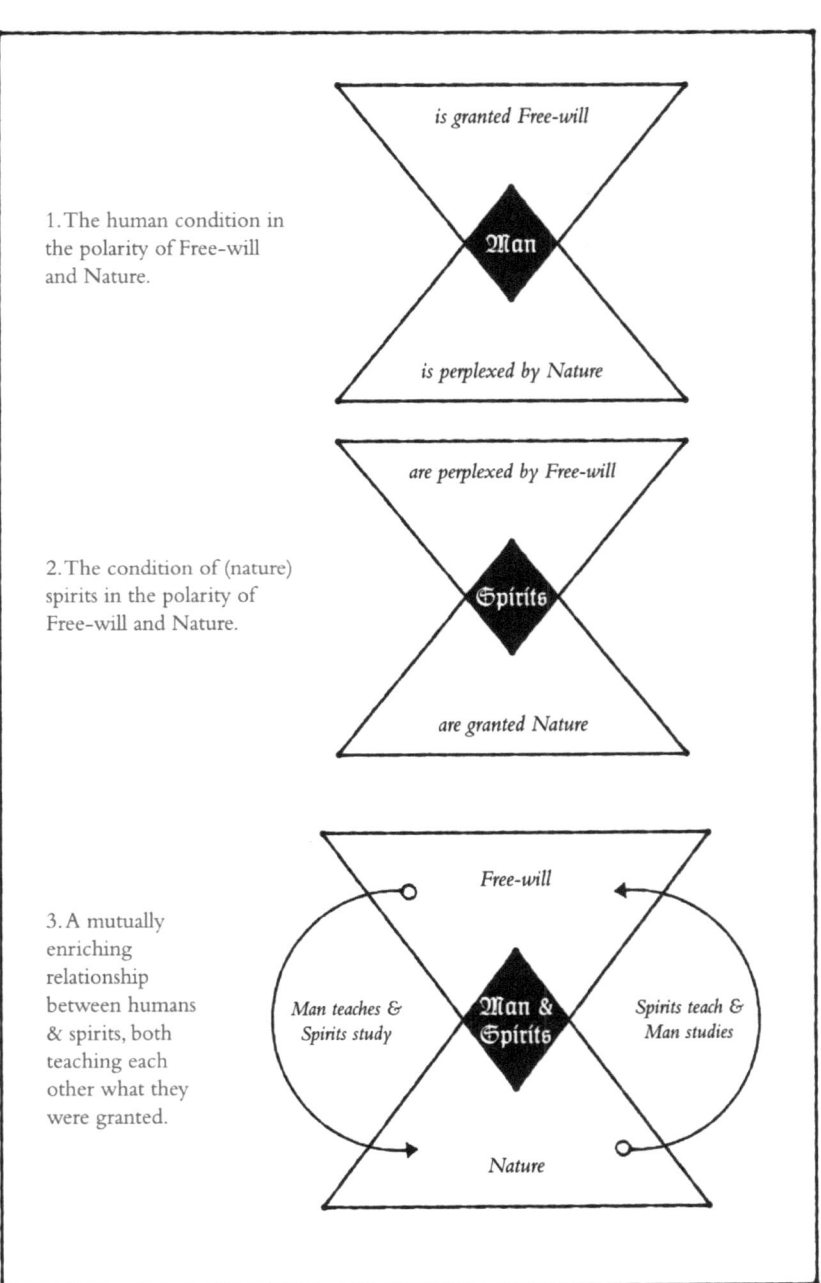

As humans we are granted free will, and yet constantly perplexed by nature. As (e.g. elementary) spirits we are granted the essence of nature, and yet constantly perplexed by humans applying free will.

What if we became both teachers and students to each other? What if humans came to see each act of applying free will as a learning blueprint for the surrounding spirits. And what if we invited the spirits teach us about nature on their own terms, in their own ways, rather than forcing our way through them with sheer will.

•

At the end of the day, Rosicrucian Magic invites us into a deeply animistic worldview.

A worldview in which we are not a distant observer or cool operator, but a swirling whirlwind of blind destruction – until we came to stand in the centre of the cross, silent, hands empty, heart open, awaiting what might happen next.

Chapter 7.

On Prudence combined with Virtue by Karl von Eckartshausen

Introduction

Since the emergence of Rock 'n' Roll in the 1950s we have all become quite familiar with the idea of the *cover version* in music. Unfortunately, that is not true yet in literature.

Many gems of wisdom remain buried in time, expressed in voices and tones that distance them from our modern times. Rather than digging them up, reinterpreting them and bringing them to light again, we pass by them on dusty shelves – and fail to unite our spirit with theirs.

Most wise things have been said before. And we could save ourselves from reading and writing a lot of mediocre books, if only we looked a little closer at the great but forgotten ones, and used our own voices to amplify the echo resounding from their pages.

The following short excerpt is precisely such a reinterpretation, a literary cover version if you like. The text in its original form spanned more than 400 pages and yet had been a hybrid by birth. We have introduced its author, Carl von Eckartshausen in Chapter 3 already. For most modern readers his name no longer conjures images of ancient lineages, masonic lodges and grimoires in smoke filled rooms – unlike the names of his 18th century contemporaries such Eliphas Levi, Count Alessandro di Cagliastro (aka Giuseppe Balsamo, 1743-1795) or Comte St.Germain (1710-1784). Now that, indeed, might be a good thing; as it might make for a less prejudiced and more unbiased encounter with the actual man and his work.

The text that forms the basis of the following excerpt was first published in 1790. Eckartshausen is humbly noted as its editor. He explains in the preface that the book presents a curated effort to bring together some essential theories on virtue and prudence in the modern world. Specifically, he refers to the French book *La veritable politique des personnes de qualite* (*The True Politic of People with Character*) as its main source; a book originally published 1700 that has seen several editions since. However, no author is named anywhere and Eckartshausen admits that while he liberally took quotes from various related works he also interspersed his own ideas and voice into the more than 400 pages. As we can see, despite its relative age, we are dealing with a book that never had a pure original form, but from the beginning only existed in its *cover* or *remixed* version.

Now, despite the French Revolution and the general instability that Europe experienced at the time, printing paper must have been in solid supply for Eckartshausen and his Munich publisher Joseph Leutner in 1790. Indeed, it would have been a welcome effort to any reader, to trim the circumlocutory and repetitive text into a succinct pamphlet capable of much greater impact. Eckartshausen's own introduction together with the first 100 paragraphs contain most of the key ideas of the book; to the modern reader 230 years later much of the rest is repetition and digression.

The much shorter text you will be reading, therefore, follows in the same footsteps Eckarthausen himself took ninety years after the publication of la veritable politique: More than two centuries later it's time for another remix, time to bring this wonderful voice back to the foreground of our journeys again. The prudence and virtue it shares could not be more important to our current times. To me, it is a stark reminder of why turning into a wolf when living among wolves simply isn't good enough.

Now, let us note that the metaphor of *the wolf* in this context is exactly that, a *symbol*. No matter all the beauty, skill and social intelligence the actual species of wolves holds, at least since Roman times the metaphor of the brutal, selfish, outlawed wolf has developed in fables, tales and stage plays of the classical West. Whether we take the ancient proverb *lupus fablis*[56] or saying *homo homini lupus est*[57], the anthropomorphic wolf had turned into the epiphany of the predatory, uncivilised force that disrespects and destroys all social bonds. Which is why on the cover emblem of Eckartshausen's book we see children cutting off wolves tails. It's a gruesome symbol for unmasking the vicious motives behind most modern politics.

Carl von Eckhartshausen.

Prudence combined with Virtue. A Remix.

The theory of prudence is an essential science for the virtuous human who lives in social states and in political circumstances. A lack of knowledge of human nature, and consequently the judgement of others according to one's own heart, often allows people to plunge into disaster, and makes them commit many mistakes against the basic rules of prudence.

Repeated experience and disappointments turn the good man wary, and small is the step from love of mankind to hatred of it. Thus, it is necessary to adopt certain theories of prudence, to safeguard the good heart against deceit and malice.

---

56 literally: *(he appears like a) wolf in the fable,* the original source of today's better known proverb *speaking of the devil*

57 Latin for *man is a wolf to man*

Yet it is hard to discover such teachings, as the majority of mankind posseses the wrong kind of cleverness, one that is generally called politics, and which in itself is nothing other than the art of deceit.

No one defiles humanity more horrendously than the false politician; just as truth and benevolence adorn the soul with splendour, so baseness and deceit deform it. Wherever such politics exist, no virtue can dwell, but its semblance alone which betrays the virtuous. The innocent impulses of the human nature are suffocated, and replaced by factitious ones. Lies and falsity create world politics. And hard is it in national states and courts to choose the middle-path, not to depart from the true prudence and never to alight on false politics.

The virtuous one will always ask: What is to do? And there is only one answer that can be given as response – that which all fine people have done before: To walk the path of virtue at the hand of prudence.

As fine as the woman is who unites true prudence with virtue, as hideous as is the character of the false politician who unites base cleverness with vice, who has no original words nor capacity to think of their own, who always turns into whatever the circumstances dictate, smiling and cowering.

And smiling and cowering they suppress and yet regret having become the tool of suppression themselves. They master the art of exploiting the noble heart to their own advantage, to do everything for themselves and nothing for others, and on the rubble of the failed luck of their neighbour they erect the throne of their own.

In the end, the high-minded will not change the world; all that is left, is to do as much good as lies within their power, and to always protect innocence with prudence.

Zeitgeist

Mankind in its essence never changes much; time and context cause the differences that separate today's people from those of centuries past. The finest, most clever gentleman of the 12th century might be quite awkward and bashful in our time.

With court and politics, things really are no different from theatre: Love and ambition are the common material of every play, and the weave of the net of intrigues differentiates the story. It is important to know the fashions of one's time.

Honour

In respect to temporality, honour is nothing but the work of man; it is nothing in and of itself. Yet through the immense span of time during which it has lived amongst mankind, it has achieved so much gravity and esteem, that its value seems to supersede most other temporal things. Thus, one cannot take care enough of one's good reputation; and bring honor to the name one received at birth.

Everything that sparkles is suspicious. Beware not to aim to excel in your mental capabilities to the detriment of your heart's voice. You did not receive your cognitive mind to sport it in public, but to use it for the good. It should shine through you, yet not be admired.

And remember in all your doing, that the way you act and the grace that accompanies your deeds, will substitute for most other things.

Yet, be strict in keeping your word, and always act upon what you have said. Frequently remind yourself of what one of the wise men of Greece once said: *Three things are required to become like a god: Doing good, speaking the truth and keeping your word.*

Honour is entirely built from virtue. Both are the only two goods entirely independent of good fortune as well as from the orders of the sovereigns.

Wisdom

Therein lies wisdom if one is neither embarrassed to talk nor to be silent. Silence not always veils great insights. The one talks the best who never talks untimely.

Self-Love

Always be wary of the unforgiving enemy called self-love. She stirs all desires and causes turmoil.

A noble naivety exists, she is the friend of all wisdom. She is most suitable to discard the errors of self-love, as she is more sublime than anything that could be acquired by study or education.

Yet our hearts know too many weaknesses, which make it easy for self-love to intrude. Everyone accounts for their own worth so much higher than it is. There is so much self-deceit in the choice of careers, as people deem themselves able to become everything that flatters their self-love and opens an unrestricted field to their desires.

So do not allow for your errors to turn grey. A long habit of co-existing with evil is always a more sovereign empress than common-sense.

Self-love slips through every crack and crevice. She is so attentive and so delicate, that irrespective of how alert you are and thoroughly you seek to know yourself, you will still overlook her here and there.

Always remember the proverb of an old Spaniard: 'A ship seems great in a river and yet is tiny at high sea.'

Shallow Minds

The world is full of shallow minds. They do not possess anything that is their own, and only live on borrowed knowledge. Endeavour to find the ones from whom speak true common-sense and thorough learning. Be mindful to act with equanimity upon their advice. Only trust talent that stems from first-hand experience.

Glory

Do not aim to stand in the seeming respect of other people; never beg for their praise. Do not search for any other glory in your deeds than the one of having done them. Do good because of the good; this is the true ground upon which your name should be built. This alone is how, over time, you will force people to respect you.

Avarice

Flee from avarice; of all vices she is the most base. The prodigal makes themselves despised, the scrooge makes themselves generally detested.

Be generous and bountiful. Imagine you would lose everything you do not give. Yet to not become a prodigal do often consult prudence for advice. There is no virtue without the latter.

The best technique to always enjoy matters of luck with inner calm, is to always be prepared to lose without grieving; that one seeks to prevent poverty, which certainly persecutes those who cannot do without the most superfluous needs.

Happiness

Do not become the weather vane of chance. Never take your sight from the main object that will lead to your happiness. Too many projects make for none of them being successful.

Make good use of the adversities in life, whenever hostile luck plunges you into them. Consider that they will sharpen your mind, and grant buoyancy and firmness, which both will strengthen and develop your courage.

Never shrink from the gravity of great virtue. Not once will she push you down to the ground. Quite the opposite, you will carry her with increasing ease the more you are laden with her.

Never raise your view so far into the future that you forget the present moment.

Friendship

Ensure that you are loved by other people, and not feared. Friendship holds ineffable benefits – an evil sign if one does not feel these.

Make friends irrespective of the costs that will come with it. Whatever they cost you, they are worth it, for as long as they are loyal and honest with you in return. However, to find such friends, you must first possess the qualities you seek for in others in yourself.

Great service done often is less relevant and less of a proof for true friendship as many small favours. Only the latter reveal how much you are really caring for your friends all the time. Great service is done with deliberation, often on purpose and more often even out of vanity. Small favours happen naturally and without any pressure applied. They gently follow the dynamics of the heart, from where they stem, and where they are governed.

But beware of befriending sentimentals; they sigh and whine in gentle elegies, yet in their actions they are as vapid as the sounds they make.

Also beware that a true friend will contradict you often, and that precisely is the testament of their unfeigned friendship. Look upon all flatterers as your enemies, who are more interested in praising your taste, then bettering your heart and illuminating your mind.

No better mirror exists than old friends. Take them for your soul doctors; accept their advice like healing potions, subject to their directive, or you will have to renounce your cure.

And remember: Scholars and wisemen in general are ragged and wild humans. They deal so much with the dead, they do not know how to dwell among the living.

Self-Knowledge

The most useful of all sciences is the one taught through self- knowledge and improvement of self. The only reason for not improving yourself further, is because you are not seeking diligently enough to know yourself better.

There is nothing we know less than than our selves. And still nothing is of graver importance with respect to ourselves than not to deceive ourselves.

The sign of a bright mind is to know how to live with oneself. Make your inner calm independent of other people just as much as of good luck. Learn how to be your own best friend at all times.

Never envy the superiority of other people's talents. Rather delight in having found your master. Love reason where it reveals itself.

Disputes

Nothing compares to the agony we inflict upon each other in disputes. Most things can be looked upon at least from two different angles. It is therefore unjust to demand everyone look from exactly the same angle as we.

In general, you struggle to find the words only if you haven't allowed yourself enough time to think carefully in the first place.

Let it be said again: One has to learn to live in peace with other people. You can hold on to your own opinion if you consider it valid, however, without discarding the opinions of others. That is unless the latter concern your honour or the reputation of your neighbours.

Loneliness

Dislike of loneliness in general is a sure proof of mediocrity. Many there are who cannot even be by themselves for half an hour without being bored. They do not know how to put the time to use, and thus become uneasy and sullen. Loneliness makes them sad; they become unbearable to themselves.

A man of solid mind knows how to turn to use every moment of life, and never are they occupied more usefully than when they are alone. And yet, we cannot forget that virtue means learning how to live among the living.

Virtue

Be it as it may: I very much recommend you the way of the outsider. Learn how to fight against the constant current of bad examples, hold your ground and hold on always and unswervingly to the good. Yet you will only succeed through the highest level of alertness: Without it all our good intentions turn to smoke, the crowd sweeps us along, and we will perish in the face of others.

Chapter 8

J.B. Kerning and the Inner Fulcrum of 'I AM'

Johann Baptist Krebs, aka JB Kerning (1774-1851)

One of nine brothers and sisters, Johan Baptist Krebs was born the son of a schoolmaster on 12th of April 1774 in the far German South-West, close to the village of Villingen. Given how much of a public life the man would lead, it is surprising how little we know of him today.

His only existing biography was written in 1902 and then gradually expanded to its final form as published in 1927 under the German title *J.B. Kerning - His Life and Writings. A biographical sketch.*[1] The author was Gottfried Buchner, a German publicist, whose publishing house *Renatus* issued many of the first editions of Kerning's little-known writings.

The booklet of the 1927 edition of this biographical sketch is extremely rare today. For this brief introduction to Kerning's work we commissioned the Württembergsche Landesbibliothek to issue a private digital scan. However, in addition to its scarcity, Buchner's sketch is problematic in several other ways:

- With only 52 pages the booklet truly isn't more than a rough sketch, and one that was written more than a generation after Kerning's death, based entirely on an oral tradition amongst his students and masonic brethren.

- Most of the little book's pages are dedicated to describing Buchner's infatuated and highly subjective interpretations of

---

1 Buchner, Gottfried; *J.B. Kerning - Sein Leben und seine Schriften*, Lorch: Renatus Verlag, 1927

both historic events as well as those occurring within Kerning's inner life and vision.

- Furthermore, Buchner had his own agenda in overtly denigrating the foundation of Kerning's work in an Occult-Masonic context, interpreting Kerning's writings within a Theosophic tradition which, of course, in its formal structure didn't exist during Kerning's lifetime.

- Finally, and most regrettably, Buchner's own flawed ideologies of conservative Christianity and overt pro-German racism bleed through and stain his interpretation of Kerning's work and motivation.

Stripping back these later additions, and enriching the narrative with a few scarce additional sources, a biographic skeleton of Kerning's outer life events emerges (see table opposite page).

What this rough timeline illustrates well enough is that Kerning led a life framed by a triangle, whose vertices might be best described as *Opera Work*, *Masonic Work* and *Visionary Work*. Neither of these three were independent of the others. His professional background as an opera singer, director and writer was fundamental to his interest in freemasonry. It resulted not only in the foundation of several lodges and Kerning's fifteen years as *Master of the Chair*[2], but more importantly in the general rehabilitation of freemasonry based upon Kerning's personal intervention in 1834 through Friedrich Wilhelm Carl[3].

To Kerning the stage of the opera was only a step away from the Masonic stage of the temple, which again was only a step away from the inner stage of his visionary practice. Most importantly to our current study, we will see that his voice training as a tenor –in particular his training in using one's voice to create resonance anywhere in one's body as well as to project sounds and their vibrations – had the most remarkable effect on his spiritual investigations as well as the related innovations he brought to modern Western Esotericism. Kerning

2 alternatively: *Worshipful Master*
3 the second king of Württemberg from 1816-1864

Abbreviated Curriculum Vitae of J.B. Kerning

12th April 1774	Birth of Johan Baptist Krebs close to Villingen in the Black Forrest
1782 - 1792	Pupil of the grammar school in Villingen and Konstanz
1793 (?)	Student of Catholic Theology at the University of Freiburg im Breisgau
1794	Change from university to full-time training as a professional opera singer
1795 - 1828	Member of the Court Opera House of Stuttgart
1804	Birth of the son Karl August who Kerning adopts together with his wife Maria Anna Krebs (1880 death of Karl August)
1812 - 1818	Founder of and teacher of a music institute aligned to the pedagogy of Pestalozzi
1820	Krebs is granted the grade of 'Knight-Apprentice' (Ritter-Lehrling) by the John's Lodge of Aries (Johannis-Loge zum Widder) in Berlin
1828 - 1851	Director and vocal pedagoge at the Court Opera House of Stuttgart
c. 1830	Krebs establishes a circle of Freemasons in Stuttgart and assumes alias J.M. Gneiding
1831 - 1840	Publication of the 'Masonic Messages' (Maurerische Mitteilungen) in six volumes
1834	Through a letter to King Wilhelm I. Krebs achieves the official end of the ban of Freemasonry in Baden which had been established since 1774
1835	Foundation of the lodge 'William to the Rising Sun in the Orient' (Wilhelm zur aufgehenden Sonne im Orient Stuttgart) as a daughter-lodge to the mother-lodge 'To the Sun in the Orient Bayreuth' (Zur Sonne im Orient Bayreuth)
1835	Krebs is elected as the 'Worshipful Master' (Meister vom Stuhl) in the Stuttgart lodge
1835 - 1846	The Stuttgart Lodge is holding its meetings in the house of the Pharmacist Haidlen at Eberhardstrasse 5 (today Augustenstrasse 11)
1837	Krebs is personally received by King Wilhelm I.
1839 - 1840	Interruption of Kreb's office as 'Worshipful Master' while his lodge-brother von Koelle is taking office
1840	von Koelle departs from the Stuttgart lodge and establishes the rival lodge 'The Ancient Three Cedars' (Die alte 3 Zedernloge)
1840, June	Krebs is elected as the 'Worshipful Master' again
1840 (?)	Krebs establishes a new grade called 'Sabbithengrad' which encompasses his occult teachings focused on letters words and sounds as divine primal forces
1841	Publication of his book 'The Freemason' (Der Freimaurer) in Dresden
1841	Krebs is granted honorary membership in the mother-lodge in Bayreuth
1841	Krebs chooses the alias J.B. KERNING
1842	Foundation of additional sister-lodges
1843	Official peace settlement with the Three Cedars lodge
1846	Active participation in the Masonic Congress in Strasbourg, 16th to 18th of August
1847	Director of the second Masonic Congress, 21st to 22nd of August
1851	Accident with head-injury
1851	Death of J.B. Krebs, aka Kerning, on 2nd of October

formally condensed these teachings on *sounds as elementary forces of the divine* in the newly founded *Sabbithengrad* which he introduced to his lodge around 1840.

It should also be stressed how strongly Kerning himself was influenced by the ideas of Johann Heinrich Pestalozzi (1746 – 1827). Pestalozzi was a Swiss pedagogue and educational reformer whose work proved to have long-lasting effect on the Swiss and German educational system in general. He promoted a revolutionary, modern, child-centred method of education, fully aligned to his motto *learning by head, hand and heart*.

At the centre of this method was the idea to raise a child holistically as a full human being as well as a mature member of the social community, rather than as a passive vessel to be filled with cognitive, formally-structured knowledge. Pestalozzi's method proposed to enable the child on a lightly guided journey of self-discovery, spanning across the four spheres of (1) home and family, (2) vocational and individual self-determination, (3) and state and nation, as well as (4) the fourth sphere, which was called 'inner sense'.

Pertaining to the latter, presuming that education had successfully enabled the individual to take care of his or her basic needs, the final step was to enable them to discover and create an environment for themselves that fostered inner peace and positive faith. The rather utopian socio-political goal of this approach was the holistic education of all people to empower every member of a community – irrespective of class or income – to work independently and yet collaboratively towards shared democratic goals.[4]

To further illustrate the nature as well as the strong influence of Pestalozzi's pedagogic work on Kerning's later occult methodology, we will present a few significant quotes from the former. These come

---

4 Pestalozzi's method was used by the cantonal school in Aarau that Albert Einstein attended, which Einstein credited with fostering his process of visualising problems and his use of thought experiments. Einstein said of his education at Aarau, 'It made me clearly realise how much superior an education based on free action and personal responsibility is to one relying on outward authority.'

from one of Pestalozzi's earliest works, *The Evening Hours of a Hermit*[5]. This short booklet, published originally in 1780 in the form of a 20-page manifest, already contained most of the revolutionary programmatic ideals that Pestalozzi turned into pedagogic practice during the second half of his life.

> *Viewpoint of life, individual self-determination of man, you are the book of nature. Within you lies the power and the order of this wise leader, and any school education that is not built on the basis of shaping human character and development is misleading.*[6]

> *The scattered tangle of multi-knowledge is no more the basis of nature. The human being, who flutters around all knowledge with light flight and who does not strengthen his knowledge by silent, firm application; he, too, loses his cheerful, attentive gaze, the quiet, truly pleasurable feeling of truth. The gait of the men is wavering, who, in the confusion of their multiplicity of knowledge, find much talking but sacrifice the quiet sense of pure human wisdom. At the noise of their pride you will find near them empty desolation and darkness, whereas under the same conditions the power of the blessed sage shines brightly.*[7]

> *Man has to be educated to acquire inner peace. Without inner peace, man falls on wild waves. Thirst and urge for impossible forms rob him of all enjoyment of the current, present blessing, as well as of every power of the wise, patient, and mindful spirit.*[8]

> *Believe in yourself, human, believe in the inner sense of your being, so you believe in God and in immortality.*[9]

---

5 Pestalozzi, Johann Heinrich; *Abendstunde eines Einsiedlers*, Fürth: Schmid, 1846 (1780)

6 Pestalozzi, p.12

7 Pestalozzi, p.17

8 Pestalozzi, p.18

9 Pestalozzi, p.23

> *I am touching strings that lie unstrung and that do not sound fashionably. Deride them, dancer-sound, trilling slander, drown their strength in your cry! Truth and pure human sense make me unconcerned.*[10]

Fully in line with Pestalozzi's manifest, Johann Baptist Krebs aspired to explore life holistically in all its facets. Over the course of his career he was a highly regarded classical tenor, composer, vocal-pedagogue, pianist, opera director, occult author and poet. His masonic and visionary work, both in writing as well as within his lodges, occupied the second half of his life; in particular the two decades from 1830 to 1850. He gained increasing profile as an occult author during these later years, and while most of his writings took the form of internal teaching letters to his masonic brethren, some of his writings [11] were published to to the general public. It was during the last decade of his life that he chose the alias *Kerning* with an eye to protecting his privacy amid the calm and humble life he led in Stuttgart.

If we believe the testament of his students, Kerning's life-long curiosity was only surpassed by his natural positivity and idealism. Against the backdrop of the significant disruptions Europe experienced during his life-time, from the French Revolution to the Napoleonic Wars and the Industrial Revolution, we can see this character trait for the exceptional quality it was. In a world that was over-throwing everything it had believed in, Kerning worked tirelessly to resurface and restore what he considered an ancient, authentic Western Mystery school.

In light of this, his work deserves particular recognition through at least three lenses: (1) In all of his writings Kerning carefully avoided the 'ego-trap'. I.e., he managed to keep his teachings free from any personal aspirations and the desire to create a pedestal either for himself as a wisdom-teacher or some kind of ancient authority. His entire opus pulls the student towards a single point: and that is to focus on the actual practical work.

---

10 Pestalozzi, p.28

11 e.g. Kerning, J.B.; *Maurerische Mitteilungen - Manuskripte für Brüder Freimaurer* Band I und II, Lorch: Karl Rohm, 1910

(2) Secondly, while his writings go into great detail in analysing the occult wisdom seemingly encrypted in the masonic symbols and rituals, Kerning avoided overlaying additional man-made structure into his teachings. No oaths have to be taken, no inner and outer circles are established, no additional titles or robes are handed out – instead his books aim to leverage a language as precise and simple as possible – and to tear down the veil that separates the foreground and background of the stage.

(3) Thirdly, and perhaps most importantly, a closer look at the body of occult techniques Kerning taught reveals him to be an active agent of advanced visionary magic in the 19th century. During the time Eliphas Levi (1810-1875) was winning fame for his highly speculative and theoretical tomes on the Tarot and the Tree of Life (only to encounter various setbacks and, not long after, largely abandon the ring of magical practice), we encounter the completely opposite pattern in Kerning. Standing in the quiet solitude of his garden in Stuttgart, we are told, he taught himself to listen and to commune with the spirits, both within the human body as well as in the vast world surrounding it.

Along with recognizing the value of Kerning's work, we should also highlight a critical remark. The genuine authenticity of the visionary system that Kerning rediscovered for his time wasn't always a perfect match with the masonic tradition and framework he chose as a vessel for his studies and teachings. Establishing a coherent reading of masonic ritual and symbology according to his visionary work and premises often results in highly speculative and subjective interpretations. Rather than lightly weaving an ancient meaning back into the fabric of the masonic lodge, in the long run such effort has to be recognised as an artificial attempt to turn freemasonry into something it was never intended to be.

> *Kerning's searching and researching mind settled into the organization and tradition of the lodge. Indeed, he inserted words and meaning into it that neither the original founders of Freemasonry had intended, nor*

> *have they been absorbed and preserved by the time after him. Kerning's freemasonry essentially was a failed attempt (...) to deepen and reform freemasonry.*[12]

What might be described as one of many failed attempts to dress freemasonry in authentic occult robes resulted nonetheless in a significant contribution to the Western Mystery tradition. The (often silent) impact of Kerning's work can be witnessed in the absorption of many of his practices and methods by prominent later occult voices such as Alois Mailänder, Gustav Meyrink, Friedrich Weinreb, Bo Yin Ra, Franz Bardon and Emil Stejnar.

J.B. Kerning's Visionary Practice

We now turn to a closer look at the actual practices Kerning advocated. A preliminary and rather raw overview of Kerning's mysto-magical system might look somewhat like this:

(1) In the first phase he taught his students to vibrate vocals and consonants in the appropriate manner. For the five vowels (respectively nine: *i, e, ä, ü, ö, ao, u, o, a*) this meant not only learning how to intone their pure, resonating sounds, but more importantly how to perceive their life-giving vibrancy in silence, or alternatively, as induced through an aligned symbolic gesture formed by one's fingers. Once these five essential life-forces bound into the sounds of the vowels were mastered, the student was guided into acquiring equal skill in intoning the consonants. This meant differentiating the consonants into Lip- (B,M,R,W), Tongue- (D,N,R,L), Teeth- (F,B,S,SCH) and Palate-Letters (G,NG,R,CH), i.e. the locations where their sounds emerge and where they achieve their greatest impact. Much attention and care was given to learning the vibration of each of these letters in their respective place – and then again to do the same in complete silence. (Note: The teeth were not considered to hold their own sound, rather they were used to produce the specific consonants.)

(2) In the second phase the student learned to make the letters

---
12 Buchner, 1927, p.12

vibrate in each human organ and, ultimately, throughout the entire body. The goal of this stage was to master and mobilise the unique vibrations of vowel- and consonant combinations throughout one's body. Specific exercises aided the evocation (silent or spoken) of vibrations in the feet, which gradually spread over the rest of the body. This practice would follow painstaking levels of detail. I.e., depending on whether one practiced as an Apprentice, Fellow or Adept, the body was divided into different intervals, all the way from 8 to 64, with the goal of being able to specifically activate and 'tune' each interval through conscious letter-practice. Only advanced Adepts would centre their practice on the stomach region.[13]

(3) The third phase switched focus from an inner-mystical approach to a more mysto-magical one. Here the advanced student was taught to look at all created things in nature as having intervals or layers that could be differentiated into Lips, Teeth, Tongue and Palate. I.e., in its most simplistic form, the surface of any given fruit would be its lips, the flesh, its tongue and the kernel its palate. More importantly, Kerning suggested that placing one's finger onto a physical object (or one's thoughts onto an immaterial object) would produce a response in the form a mouth at this particular place through which it spoke back to the human.[14] Accordingly, Kerning not only aimed to enliven the spiritual body of the practitioner, but he aimed to empower his advanced students with an authentic Western animistic tradition: He offered a pathway for the spirit world to respond to human touch, an occult path that allowed adepts to weave themselves back into the fabric of nature – all guided by the life-creating forces and vibrations of inner and outer utterances.

Before examining in greater detail specific techniques of Kerning's practice, we will take a moment to listen to his own voice. Here are a series of significant quotes, taken from his most influential book

---

13 While Kerning stressed that his unique way of segmenting the human body into as many as 64 intervals did not follow the same principle as a musical scale, one clearly detects Kerning's training as a professional opera singer in this work.

14 We might want to remember Paracelsus' quote in Chapter 2 on the self-created spirits generated from will.

Letters on the Royal Art (*Briefe über die Königliche Kunst*, Renatus Verlag 1912), which was originally published in a limited and numbered edition for the purpose of borrowing it to students only.

About Freemasonry & being human

Freemasonry during its good times, when one did not tie it to any time, history or person, only had one purpose, to awaken the word within and to be educated by it on the purpose and duties of creation. Once one aimed to tie our institution to a history, a country, or to a person, it ceased to be a wisdom school and turned into a pietist-institute with rationalist make-up.[15]

Man shall have the courage to either deny everything and to discard the dignity of mankind, or alternatively, where one is handed the tools like it is the case here, they shall make the test; then they will be either cold or warm. In the half-assed belief and indifference, however, into which man has sunken, they are lukewarm and necessarily have to be disgorged.[16]

The fallacy that continuously leads to further fallacies, consist thereof that one regards wisdom as the highest quality of God. Such claim is in no way better as when the rationalist claims: God is the purest rationality. Wisdom and reason are lights which one may own, but both of which require an owner.[17]

Sign, grasp, word - seeing, feeling, hearing. [...] As sign, grasp and word can be exercised upon us without the aid of any outer objects, man contains an entire world within himself, in which he can continuously gather new experiences and insights.[18]

As important as the way of acquiring insight may be, it is nevertheless the one of which we have the least clear understanding. The bound

---

15 Kerning, *Briefe*, p. 87
16 Kerning, *Briefe*, p. 14
17 Kerning, *Briefe*, p. 20
18 Kerning, *Briefe*, p. 14/16

man, intimidated by many doctrinal systems, has always been afraid and is still afraid of a teaching which points man back to himself, and which shows him the tools to realize the spirit on a technical path, to approach God and to obtain the laws of life and immortality.[19]

Shame has turned many honest men dishonest. [...] Not from the outside comes the darkening, but from the inside.[20]

About the Inner Person & Immortality

The outer man with his knowledge and agency cannot achieve a positive kind of immortality. For this it is necessary that he must be able to speak his 'I', his name at heart, in all his organs of his body, may they be on the inside or outside, and that he may hear these organs speaking back to him in return. If the soul and its spirit get stuck in our flesh and blood, and fail to enliven themselves to become a free 'I', they are still buried in the earth, and when the dissolution comes they as well will have to dissolve into atoms. As soon as we have freed them of their captivity and made them speak, they will absorb the outer 'I' into themselves, they will become master and ruler even of our mortal life, and once we have become one with them they will guide us towards immortality in triumph. For this reason it is our essential duty to make our soul speak, to put ourselves into dialogue with it, and to receive from it the infallible laws for our actual existence. So fresh to work! Initially we are the teacher of the spirit and the soul; however, once they begin to feel their own powers, they turn into the teacher and we into the disciples, who can rely upon their protection and guidance just like the plants rely on the influence of the sun. That is why the spirit shall dictate the words to me, so they may merge into your soul with their fertilising powers and to enrich you with all the treasures of eternity.[21]

---

19 Kerning, *Briefe*, p. 152

20 Kerning, *Briefe*, p. 101/102

21 Kerning, *Briefe*, p. 85

The tones of music through their vibration form certain kinds of lines. The vibration of the vowels is bound to particular rules; once their vibration is interrupted through consonants and united with these, a richness of effects is created that cannot be counted.[22]

The vocals, on which the apprentice has to train, are nothing but life, they are life-currents, which neither hold a beginning nor an end, nor know stagnation. The consonants create the intercessions into these currents, and in order not to always flow in straight or crooked paths, they lend them angles and breaks, and thus grant character and meaning to a language. This is how the apprentice shall learn to feel life, by aiming to think of the vocals in the palate and in their mouth and by processing them in such a way that they flow down to their feet in order to spread into their entire body from there. Once this has happened, the fellow walks with the sign on their chest, they close their lips, tongue and even partly their palate and initially aim to feel the Lip-Letters on their lips, the Tongue-Letters on their tongue, and the Palate-Letters on their palate, and to lower them down into the body, into their stomach, almost as if they were nutrients to be spread throughout the entire body. Tedious and painstaking of course is this work; yet man may not be frightened by trouble and challenge, as they know these are the only way to soar and strengthen themselves.[23]

Up until now we have perceived the palate in the center of our I, of our gestalt. We were the place from where our journey started and with lip and tongue, with M and N we have orbited creation, only to descend from the largest to the smallest circle, and so were able to realize the spirit of creation. Yet man may soar even higher; he can start from himself as the palate and then position it out into eternity, and allow tongue and lips to orbit at will. Man is capable, from wherever he drew a border through lip and tongue, to advance even further; and to inverse the act in the equivalent distance to where he is positioned towards the circles, and to create a palate, an I, at the opposite end; and thus listen to the teaching and the answer of the Word from borderless

---

22 Kerning, *Briefe*, p. 136

23 Kerning, *Briefe*, p. 41

> *distance. [...] In this manner nature is enlivened for man, as if he was surrounded by geniuses.*[24]
>
> *So we do not want to be timid, but spell it or even say say spells until the ribs crack and then dare to enter the master's cabin with joyful courage.* (Kerning, Briefe, p.43)

The Root Exercise : Introduction

It is hoped that, in the absence of first-hand experience to elaborate upon it, the above overview contains sufficient insights and guidance that the curious practitioner can carve their own path into *the art of turning letters into flesh*.

Two correlations to later magical currents, however, should be pointed out here before we advance: In most 20th century magical systems, such as the canon of *Golden Dawn* teachings, the idea of vibrating divine names takes a prominent place. It is leveraged as a central ritual technique to activate both the spiritual and physical realms through the proper application of the sound of the human voice. Secondly, much of the magical works of Austin Osman Spare (1886-1956) pivot on the idea of *turning words into flesh*. Both techniques not only gain historic, but more importantly practical depth, when also studied through the lens of Kerning's system. Revolving entirely around the idea of weaving letters and words into flesh, of using their original sounds to activate and draw out the dormant spiritual consciousness within our organic cells, Kerning's teachings are as timeless as they are foundational to the magical work of many an advanced practitioner.

Now, while I do not have extensive experience with Kerning's full system, I have practiced a subset of his techniques for more than twenty years. In fact, unconscious of their original source, these were the first practices I came across on my magical path in this life.

Here is how this happened: One of the most influential 20th

---

[24] Kerning, *Briefe*, p. 138

century occult authors in the German speaking countries was the above-mentioned novelist Gustav Meyrink (1868-1932). A member of a wide array of magical lodges and mystical circles of his time, both in Europe and in Asia, Meyrink pursued an almost obsessively adamant and rigorous personal solo practice. Famous are the stories of his night-long asana meditations on a cold park bench in Prague, the rigidness with which he pursued Kerning's as well as Indian tantric practices to the letter, as well as the Saturnian decidedness with which he would dismiss techniques, after devoting years of ardent focus to them, if they ultimately failed to deliver the expected results. Asked why, when equipped with all these experiences and insights, he would only write occult novels rather than occult-study manuals or non-fiction books on related topics, Meyrink's answer was sharp and clear: Firstly, not everyone was ready to start their journey by reading the equivalent of Goethe's Faust; most people needed a gentler path towards the other side. Secondly, and more importantly, his novels actually weren't intended to speak to the conscious mind of the reader. Instead, he wrote all of them in a spiritually channeled manner and had constructed them to work as narrative sigils, reaching for contact with the dormant, inner self of his readers.

Meyrink's novels were the first books I read as a young man. At least on myself the intended impact was not lost. Indeed, his novels worked for me like the proverbial key slotted into the keyhole. Not only did his books show me the inner, mystical path I would follow for the next twenty-five years, more importantly they helped me discover the inner voice that would guide and advise me on this path. With the exception of Josephine McCarthy's liminal works, no other magical books have ever had the same effect on me. At the time, however, I did not know from which occult sources Meyrink himself had taken the ideas and voices he brought to life in his novels. As it turned out, the works of J.B.Kerning were among the most prominent influences on his own practice and literary creations.

In many of Meyrink's novels we are introduced to the idea that man was created in the shape of a Janus-head: With one face of his dual human nature looking at the sensual, outer world, and another, second and hidden face peering deep into the inner realm.

According to Meyrink, in most people's lives, however, the latter, inward looking face is never awakened from its slumber and instead keeps its eyelids firmly closed from cradle to grave.[25]

To Meyrink, magic in all its forms was a means of achieving essentally two things: In its first phase, to switch consciousness from the outward looking face to its inward looking twin - to help raise one's inner eyelids, sharpen one's view and help create familiarity with the inner world. In its second phase, one even less frequently achieved by adepts, the goal was to raise one's eyelids of both faces at once – and to be consciously present both in the inner and outer realm at the same moment in time.

'Together on either side' (*Hueben und drueben zugleich*) was the straightforward magical motto Meyrink coined for this awakened state of adept consciousness; the ultimate goal of his own occult life's journey.

Now, how directly this central idea of Meyrink's oeuvre is related to Kerning's mystical teachings we can see from the following quotes:

> *Two selves reveal themselves in the magnetized, an external and an internal. When the external ceases to be active, the inner becomes effective, and vice versa; if the inner is not effective, the external senses open.*[26]

> *Now one wonders whether it would not be possible to imagine the magnetized state as permanent, so that the human being reflected and decided with their inner ego, and used the external only for mundane activities? (…) Yes, in this way the human being would become a truly unique species indeed, whose needs arise from the spirit and whose animal nature served as a basis for processing his spiritual powers.*[27]

---

25 We might want to recall Paracelsus' notion of an inner firmament, and individuals living their lives with measure and aim.

26 Kerning, *Der Schlüssel zur Geisterwelt*, p. 17

27 Kerning, *Der Schlüssel zur Geisterwelt*, p. 18

> *Two selves belong to the human being, an external and internal one. While the latter man departs from the hand of the Creator; the former is given to him by the world; and how powerful this latter self affects him can be deduced from this: that most people have no trace, even no idea of an inner, spiritual and free life anymore.*[28]

> *Man belongs to two worlds, the temporal and the eternal. Whoever lives the first alone will never know the second. But whoever wanted to surrender himself to the second, would clog up manifold sources of knowledge. Both belong to man, for both he holds duties; only when he fulfills them will the true light, the light of eternity, appear to him and show him the path of immortality, which he is destined to walk by the Creator.*[29]

Meyrink was born seventeen years after Kerning's death. However, a contemporary of both Kerning and Meyrink formed another strong link in the chain. Carl du Prel (1839-1899) was a widely read philosopher, occultist and mystical author of the 19th century. In one of his major works The Philosophy of Mysticism (Die Philosophie der Mystik, 1855) we come across the exact same perspective on the inner human constitution:

> *So, hidden from our self-consciousness, there lies a transcendental subject in the background of our being, the root of our individuality; it differs from our outwardly focussed, sensory self by form and and content of knowledge, because it is woven into nature in different ways, i.e. it receives other impressions from nature, that is to say, organically it reacts to them in a different way than the sensual person.*[30]

From a historic perspective, it has to be stressed that much of the research, experimentation and occult philosophies of Kerning, du Prel and Meyrink were energised less by forms of traditional magic or sorcery than by the phenomena described by Mesmerism, Animal Magnetism, Spiritism and early forms of hypnosis. The 19th century

---

28 Kerning, *Der Schlüssel zur Geisterwelt*, p. 20
29 Kerning, *Grundzüge der Bibel*, p.7
30 Carl du Prel, *Philosophie der Mystik*, p. 462

followed on the heels of a period of radical secularisation that ultimately unleashed and led to the perfect storm of aggressive industrialisation, unprecedented urbanisation and the dominance of the young objective sciences. Across large parts of Europe the foundations of traditional folk-belief were wiped away just as thoroughly as was the socially embedded, unquestioned dominance of Christianity. During these deeply disruptive times, occultists aimed to join the newly emerging mainstream in probing the psychology and inner dynamics of the human being.

Today, we hold the privilege of choosing whether to stand in a less radical and more balanced position. Almost 200 years later, we have witnessed both the good and the bad, the radical gains and the desperate losses that followed in the shadows of industrialisation and which have resulted in the extreme exploitation of nature and the continued degradation of rural communities. Similarly, we also can choose to assume a more balanced viewpoint on traditional systems of magic: While deeply constrained by man-made boundaries, forms and rites which were passed on for centuries mainly by male dominated groups, in part still act as ancient vessels not only of spiritual wisdom, but also of practical techniques that continue to hold significant value even in the modern world.

This increased ability to recognise complexity and paradox and to choose our position accordingly, is one of the main advantages of our modern time. Unfortunately, it is one that is realised much too infrequently. And yet, we can choose to be far less bound by unquestioned social norms, authorities, habits, and one-dimensional ways of weighing gains versus losses, than our ancestors ever had the chance to be. Kerning did not speak the language of *theurgy* or *goêteia*, but of a human-centred mysticism. Meyrink used his own language to conjure up forgotten forms and voices in our imagination and dreams. What will your language be?

The essential question, when beginning to work with the following root exercise, is not whether it opens doors to an inner realm of living spirits, or to a previously dormant psychological side of our selves, or even to a mathematical dimension that our human sense will never be fully able to understand. Whichever side of Frater U∴D∴'s critical model of magic we chose as our 'home-paradigm' – what matters is not how we choose to look at the world, but *how it responds back to us*. As Frater U∴D∴ has explained for many decades now, approaching our work with an absolute sense of pragmatism is what matters most. Whatever stops us from moving ahead is a block that deserves demolition, or even better, agile avoidance. Most often what is holding us back from truly advancing on our magical path is not something outside of ourselves, but limitations imposed by our own minds alone.

The following exercise is a powerful technique to get us unstuck, to open us up, to take ground and to centre ourselves outside of our eternally flawed, beautiful mortal selves.

The Root Exercise - Practice

Phase 1: Wherever you are, lying or standing, in public or private, close your eyes and calm your breath. Become aware of your body, in this present moment: feel your bones effortlessly upholding your form, your muscles effortlessly upholding your bones, your blood effortlessly upholding your muscles and organs, and your skin without effort upholding your outer shape. Become aware of the fine line between inside and outside. Do not strain your mind, just allow your bodily awareness to come to the foreground.

Phase 2: Allow your mind to descend to your feet. Like a stone thrown into a lake, your consciousness is sinking through your body towards the soles of your feet. When it has fallen all the way to the bottom of your being, hold it gently there. Now vibrate the sound of the vowels, and feel the sound emerge from the bottom of your feet. While you do this, visualise the shape of the letters appearing on your soles, remaining there for as long as you vibrate their sounds – be playful. Vibrate and visualise a single vowel for a few minutes. Build a chain of vowels and allow them to flow. But always keep your vibration and visualisation in sync, i.e., continue to "see" the respective shape of the vowel you are intoning on your soles. Practice in silence, feeling the sound of the letters in your body and mind only, as well as with your real voice in different pitches. Discover what works best for you.

Phase 3: When your feet feel warm and alive from the sounding of the vowels, slowly allow your consciousness to rise. Like an air bubble rising under water, this happens without effort. Your consciousness moves slowly through your legs, your groin, your stomach, until it arrives in your chest. In the centre of your heart it comes to rest for a moment. You realise, there is a light here. A golden, radiating light. Allow your consciousness to rest and relax in its presence, observing the shine and brilliance as it fills your chest.

Phase 4: When your consciousness has become saturated with light, simply observe as it rises up further, into the upper part of your chest and into the base of your neck. Arriving at your throat, as if taken by a light breeze, your consciousness turns at a 90-degree angle to move toward the back of your body. It emerges from your skin roughly at the spot between your throat and the top of your scapulas. Here, it moves further out, until it comes to rest at a point approximately 20cm or 8 inches behind you. Just as you did in your soles and heart area, gently hold your consciousness in presence here. Then, in this place slightly behind and outside of your physical body, vibrate the words *'I AM'*. – Be curious as to what effect this last phase has for you. It might change over time. See how long you can stay present in this place behind your shoulders, anchored lightly in the sound of *'I AM'*. Once you have trained for a while, feel free to expand the thought into the silent mantra of: *'I AM a soul. I HAVE a body. I AM FREE to choose.'*

Please note, there is nothing orthodox about this exercise. It has moved through many hands and taken slightly different forms each time. From Kerning to Meyrink to Emil Stejnar and now to you, it will continue to morph over time. Personally, I call it my 'root exercise' because it is the most straight forward and versatile exercise I have come across for centering myself in a stable place.

Nothing will ever be able to shake the consciousness waiting for you in this spot behind your shoulder blades when you enter it anchored in the presence of 'I AM'. It is there, eternally present, behind the veil of your skin, outside the stream of your blood. It hovers beyond the reach of any physical sickness, emotional turmoil or swing of moods. It simply, always is. And your way to it is always open.

Once you have sufficient practice in the root exercise, it will be easy to activate the consciousness in the spot roughly 20cm behind your shoulder-blades at any moment in time. This will become a matter of a split second, the way your mind re-orientates in a split second when someone calls you by name. And one day, you may find yourself hearing none other than your Holy Daimon calling from this place.

Portrait of Johann Baptist Krebs, aka Kerning, source: Georg Buchner, *J.B. Kerning - Eine biographische Skizze*, Lorch: Renatus 1902

Bibliography

- Acher, Frater; *Black Abbot White Magic, Johannes Trithemius and the Angelic Mind*, London: Scarlet Imprint, 2020
- Acher, Frater; *Clavis Goêtica*, Keighley: Hadean Press, 2021
- Acher, Frater; *Holy Daimon*, London: Scarlet Imprint, 2018
- Acher, Frater; *Holy Heretics*, London: Scarlet Imprint, 2021
- Acher, Frater; *On the Order of the Asiatic Brethren*, 2015, https://theomagica.com/on-the-asiatic-brethren-ebook
- Andreae, Johann Valentin: *Gesammelte Schriften Band 2: Nachrufe, Autobiographische Schriften, Cosmoxenus*, Stuttgart-Bad Cannstatt: frommann-holzboog, 1995
- Andreae, Johann Valentin; *Gesammelte Schriften Band 3: Rosenkreuzerschriften*, Stuttgart-Bad Cannstatt: frommann-holzboog, 2010
- Andreae, Johann Valentin; *Gesammelte Schriften Band 5: Theca Gladii Spiritus*, Stuttgart-Bad Cannstatt: frommann-holzboog, 2003
- Assmann, Jan; *Ma'at. Gerechtigkeit und Unsterblichkeit im Alten Ägypten*, München: C.H. Beck, 2006
- Assmann, Jan; *The Mind of Egypt: History and Meaning in the Time of the Pharaohs*, trans. Andrew Jenkins, Cambridge, Mass.: Harvard University Press, 2003
- Betz, Hans-Dieter (ed.); *The Greek Magical Papyri in Translation*, Volume One: Texts, Chicago: University of Chicago Press, 1992
- Beyer, Bernahrd; *Das Lehrsystem des Ordens der Gold- und Rosenkreuzer*, Leipzig: Pansophie Verlag, 1925

- Beyer, Bernhard; *Das Freimaurer-Museum*, Band 1-7. Archiv für reimaurerische Ritual-Kunde und Geschichts-Forschung. In zwangloser Folge herausgegeben vom Geschichtlichen Engbund des Bayreuther Freimaurer-Museums. Handschrift für Brr Meister, 1925-1931

- Bibliotheca Klossiana; http://www.freimaurerloge-zur-einigkeit-frankfurt.de/?seite=logenarchiv

- Brann, Noel L.; *Trithemius and Magical Theology: A Chapter in the Controversy over Occult Studies in Early Modern Europe*, Albany, NY: State University of New York Press, 1999

- Brecht, Martin; *Johann Valentin Andreae 1585-1854, Eine Biographie*, Göttingen: Vandenhoeck & Ruprecht, 2008

- Buchner, Gottfried; *J.B. Kerning - Sein Leben und seine Schriften*, Lorch: Renatus Verlag, 1927

- Dehn, Georg (ed.); *Abraham ben Simeon of Worms, The Book of Abramelin – A New Translation*, Lake Worth: Ibis Press, 2015

- Eckartshausen, Karl von; *Die Wolke über dem Heiligthum*, München, 1802, https://opacplus.bsb-muenchen.de/title/BV001410216

- Eckartshausen, Karl von; *Gott ist die reinste Liebe*, München: Lentner, 1790

- Eckartshausen, Karl von; *God is the Love most Pure*, London: Hatchard, 1817

- Ecker, Hans Karl von; *Der Rosenkreuzer in seiner Blösse: Zum Nutzen der Staaten hingestellt durch Zweifel wider die wahre Weisheit der so genannten ächten Freymäurer oder goldnen Rosenkreutzer des alten Systems*, von Magister Pianco, vieler Kreisen Bundsverwandten, Amsterdam, Nürnberg, 1781

- Frick, Karl R.H.; *Die Erleuchteten* (Teil 1), Graz: Akademische Druck- und Verlagsanstalt, 1973

- Geffarth, Renko D.; *Religion und Arkane Hierarchie: Der Orden der Gold- und Rosenkreuzer als Geheime Kirche im 18. Jahrhundert*, London, Boston: Brill, 2007

- Gikatilla, Joseph; *Gates of Light: Sha'are Orah*, translated and with an introduction by Avi Weinstein, San Francisco: Harper Collins, 1994

- Gilly, Carlos; *Adam Haslmayr - Der erste Verkünder der Manifeste der Rosenkreuzer,* Amsterdam: In de Pelikaan, 1994

- Gilly, Carlos; *ARBATEL De magia veterum. Il primo prontuario di magia bianca in Germania - The first book of white magic in Germany*, in: Carlos Gilly & Cis van Heertum (ed.), *Magia, alchimia, scienza dal '400 al '700: l'influsso di Ermete Trismegisto/ Magic, alchemy and science 15th-18th centuries: the influence of Hermes Trismegistus*, 2 volumes, Firenze, Centro Di, 2002, (Vol.1, pp. 219-240)

- Gilly, Carlos; *Khunrath und das Entstehen der frühneuzeitlichen Theosophie*, in: Heinrich Khunrath, *Amphitheatrum Sapientiae Aeternae* – Schauplatz der ewigen allein wahren Weisheit, Stuttgart-Bad Cannstatt: frommann-holzboog, 2014

- Gilly, Carlos, van der Kooij, Pleun (ed.); *Fama Fraternitas - Das Urmanifest der Rosenkreuzer Bruderschaft zum ersten Mal nach den Manuskripten bearbeitet, die vor dem Erstdruck von 1614 entstanden sind*, Haarlem: Rozekruis Pers, 1998

- Hanegraaff, Wouter J. (ed.); *Dictionary of Gnosis & Western Esotericism*, Leiden: Brill, 2006

- Horneffer, August; *Symbolik der Geheimbünde*, Heidelberg: Niels Kampmann Verlag, 1924

- Kerning, J.B.; *Briefe über die königliche Kunst*, Lorch: Renatus Verlag, 1912

- Kerning, J.B.; *Grundzüge der Bibel,* Lorch: Renatus, 1928

- Kerning, J.B.; *Lichtstrahlen vom Orient - Philosophische Betrach-*

tungen für Freimaurer, Leipzig: Wilhelm Friedrich Verlag, 1899

- Kerning, J.B.; *Maurerische Mitteilungen - Manuskripte für Brüder Freimaurer* Band I und II, Lorch: Karl Rohm, 1910

- Kerning, J.B.; *Schlüßel zur Geisterwelt - Oder die Kunst des Lebens*, Lorch: Renatus Verlag, 1926

- Kerning, J.B.; *Wege zur Unsterblichkeit - auf unleugbare Kräfte der menschlichen Natur gegründet*, Lorch: Renatus Verlag, 1936

- Lichtheim, Miriam; *Ancient Egyptian Literature Volume 1: The Old and Middle Kingdoms*, Berkeley: University of California Press, 1973

- Martin, Michael (ed.); *The Chymical Wedding of Christian Rosenkreutz - The Ezekiel Foxcroft translation revised, and with two new essays by Michal Martin*, Brooklyn, NY: Angelico Press, 2019

- Marx, Arnold; *Die Gold- und Rosenkreuzer – Ein Mysterienbund des ausgehenden 18. Jahrhunderts*, in: Bernhard Beyer, Das Freimaurer-Museum, Band V, 1930, p. 1-169

- McCarthy, Josephine; *The Quareia Apprentice Study Guide*, Exeter: Quareia Publishing UK, 2018, https://www.quareia.com/texts

- Nettelbladt, C.C.F.W. von; *Geschichte Freimaurerischer Systeme in England, Frankreich und Deutschland*, Berlin: Ernst Siegfried Mittler & Sohn, 1879

- Ozment, Steven; *The Age of Reform 1250-1550: An Intellectual and Religious History of Late Mediaeval and Reformation Europe*, New Haven & London: Yale University Press, 1980

- Pestalozzi, Johann Heinrich; *Abendstunde eines Einsiedlers*, Fürth: Schmid, 1846 (1780)

- Peuckert, Will-Erich; *Das Rosenkreutz*, Berlin: Erich Schmidt Verlag, 1973

- Peuckert, Will-Erich (ed.); *Paracelsus Werke, Studienausgabe in fünf Bänden*, Basel: Schwabe Verlag, 1965 (2010)

- Phoebron [Bernhard Joseph Schleiß von Löwnefeld]; *Der im Lichte der Wahrheit strahlende Rosenkreutzer*, Leipzig: Christian Gottlieb Hilscher, 1782

- Pistorius, Johannes; *Ars Cabalistica*, Henricpetri, Basel 1587, https://reader.digitale-sammlungen.de//resolve/display/bsb10142691.html

- Prel, Dr. Carl du; *Philosophie der Mystik,* Leipzig: Max Altmann, 1910

- Raeder, Siegfried; *Jakob Andreae und die Reformation in Wiesensteig, Öttingen und Wachendorf*, in: Hermle, Siegfried (ed.); *Reformationsgeschichte Württembergs in Porträts*, Holzgerlingen: Hänssler Verlag, 1999; https://www.wkgo.de/personen/reformationsgeschichte-in-portrts#note-273-1

- Ritman, Joost R.; *Die Geburt der Rosenkreuzerbruderschaft in Tübingen, in: Rosenkreuz als europäisches Phänomen im 17. Jahrhundert*, Amsterdam: In de Pelikaan, 2002, p. 57-74

- Roloff, Dietrich; *Gottähnlichkeit, Vergöttlichung und Erhöhung zu seligem Leben*, Berlin: De Gruyter, 1970

- Scholem, Gershom; *Die jüdische Mystik in ihren Hauptströmungen*, Frankfurt am Main: Suhrkamp, 2000

- Spunda, Franz (ed.); *Magische Unterweisungen des edlen und hochgelehrten Philosophie und Medici Philippi Theophrasti Bombastisch von Hohenheim / Paracelsus genannt*, Wolkenwanderer Verlag, 1923

- Studion, Simon; *Naometria, Teil 1*, s.l., 1604, 205 pages, in: Württembergische Landesbibliothek, Cod.theol.et.phil. qt.23,a; http://swb.bsz-bw.de/DB=2.1/PPNSET?PPN=148197517X

- Studion, Simon; *Naometria, Teil 2*, s.l., 1604, 1790 pages, in: Württembergische Landesbibliothek, Cod.theol.et.phil. qt.23,b; http://swb.bsz-bw.de/DB=2.1/PPNSET?P-PN=1481975412

- Sudhoff, Karl (ed.); *Theophrast von Hohenheim, gen. Paracelsus, Sämtliche Werke, Band 1-14*, München und Berlin: R. Oldenbourg, 1922-1933

- Tassara, S., González-Jiménez, J.M., Reich, M. et al.; *Plume-subduction interaction forms large auriferous provinces*, in: Nat Commun 8, 843, 2017, https://doi.org/10.1038/s41467-017-00821-z

- Waite, Arthur Edward; *The Brotherhood of the Rosy Cross - A History of the Rosicrucians*, Secaucus, New Jersey: University Books, 1973

- Wandrey, Irina; *'Das Buch des Gewandes' und 'Das Buch des Aufrechten'*, Tübingen: Mohr Siebeck, 2004

- Welling, Georg von; *Opus mago-cabbalisticum et theologicum. Vom Ursprung und Erzeugung des Salzes, dessen Natur und Eigenschaft, wie auch dessen Nutz und Gebrauch*, Frankfurt, 1735

- Worms, Abraham von; *Buch der wahren Praktik in der uralten göttlichen Magie*, Cologne: Peter Hammer, (1725)

Judge Softly

by Mary T. Lathrap, 1895

Pray, don't find fault with the man that limps,
Or stumbles along the road.
Unless you have worn the moccasins he wears,
Or stumbled beneath the same load.

There may be tears in his soles that hurt
Though hidden away from view.
The burden he bears placed on your back
May cause you to stumble and fall, too.

Don't sneer at the man who is down today
Unless you have felt the same blow
That caused his fall or felt the shame
That only the fallen know.

You may be strong, but still the blows
That were his, unknown to you in the same way,
May cause you to stagger and fall, too.

Don't be too harsh with the man that sins.
Or pelt him with words, or stone, or disdain.
Unless you are sure you have no sins of your own,
And it's only wisdom and love that your heart contains.

For you know if the tempter's voice
Should whisper as soft to you,
As it did to him when he went astray,
It might cause you to falter, too.

Just walk a mile in his moccasins
Before you abuse, criticize and accuse.
If just for one hour, you could find a way
To see through his eyes, instead of your own muse.

I believe you'd be surprised to see
That you've been blind and narrow-minded, even unkind.
There are people on reservations and in the ghettos
Who have so little hope, and too much worry on their minds.

Brother, there but for the grace of God go you and I.
Just for a moment, slip into his mind and traditions
And see the world through his spirit and eyes
Before you cast a stone or falsely judge his conditions.

Remember to walk a mile in his moccasins
And remember the lessons of humanity taught to you by your elders.
We will be known forever by the tracks we leave
In other people's lives, our kindnesses and generosity.

Take the time to walk a mile in his moccasins.

www.ingramcontent.com/pod-product-compliance
Lightning Source LLC
Chambersburg PA
CBHW042259280426
43661CB00108BA/1329/J